PRAISE FOR *ONE PERFECT PITCH* AND MARIE PERRUCHET

"*Perruchet's method is precise, effective, and easily replicable. Packed with useful examples and exercises,* One Perfect Pitch *is the most comprehensive guide to telling a captivating business stroy in Silicon Valley or elsewhere.*"

—GINA BIANCHINI, Founder and CEO,
Mightybell

"*This book goes straight to the fundamentals and gives you the shortcut to your perfect pitch. It clearly describes every aspect and medium of the pitching process, with helpful suggestions on what to do. The simplest and most effective book I have ever read on the subject.*"

—PAUL KIM, CTO, Stanford Graduate
School of Education

"One Perfect Pitch *provides concrete examples of how to jump-start your new pitch or improve your existing one. Whether you're preparing for a presentation to investors or chatting with a friend about your latest project, knowing how to share your story is a creative skill that requires a balance of art and science.*"

—ANNIE LEE, Content Marketing Lead,
Pinterest

"A very useful handbook for a successful pitch, starting with how to capture the attention of targeted companies and continuing to how to substantiate the contents of the pitch. Valuable anecdotes make for pleasant reading."

—JING ZHOU TAO, Managing Partner, Dechert LLP

"In a world increasingly fueled by the likes of Y Combinator, TechCrunch, and TED, the ability to communicate quickly and cleanly is a modern-day entrepreneurial necessity. One Perfect Pitch presents a unique and pragmatic perspective on how you can become successful in this important arena—so you can spend more time growing your business!"

—TOM LEE, Founder and CEO, One Medical Group

"The most compelling pitches are true to who you are. One Perfect Pitch will help you distill and share that truth for a successful business outcome."

—STÉPHANIE HOSPITAL, Cofounder, One Ragtime

"This invaluable road map provides clear, practical step-by-step directions on how to craft and deliver the perfect pitch by tapping your most important resource—you."

—JÉRÔME TERNYCK, CEO, SmartRecruiters

"*Life is a pitch. Your ability to persuade is your most powerful asset. Pitching skills can be honed. Marie's method and practical examples will show you how and draw out the best in you.*"

—FRANCOIS MAZOUDIER, CEO,
Tech Leaders Capital

"*Before we met Marie, we didn't know where to start our pitch. If you can't sell your idea, you can't survive in Silicon Valley. Marie gave us the confidence to pitch our startup effectively and secure a strategic alliance. Read* One Perfect Pitch *and see your pitch improve exponentially.*"

—SUSHEL BIJGANATH, CEO, Learnship

"*At the heart of a great pitch is an unforgettable story. Marie's expert guidance helped us tell ours. She was our competitive advantage.* One Perfect Pitch *could be yours.*"

—SUVEEN SAHIB, Cofounder, TeleportHQ, and
COO, AQUIS

"*A straight-to-the-point and fresh view on how ideas and stories are shared. This book will help you stand out.*"

—JOSE IGNACIO FERNANDEZ,
CTO, Traity

"*Whether you are starting a business, trying to pitch a new idea within your organization, or trying to ace an upcoming job interview, if you can't craft a compelling story and make an emotional connection with your audience, your product, idea, or candidacy will likely be DOA. One Perfect Pitch equips you with the proper tools and shows you how to use them successfully. Read it and reread it so that your pitch grabs and keeps your audience's attention.*"

—JOHN DAIS, former Head of Finance, Zenefits

ONE
PERFECT
PITCH

ONE PERFECT PITCH

HOW TO SELL YOUR IDEA, YOUR PRODUCT, YOUR BUSINESS—OR YOURSELF

MARIE PERRUCHET

NEW YORK   CHICAGO   SAN FRANCISCO   ATHENS
LONDON   MADRID   MEXICO CITY   MILAN
NEW DELHI   SINGAPORE   SYDNEY   TORONTO

1 2 3 4 5 6 7 8 9 0   DOC/DOC   1 2 1 0 9 8 7 6

ISBN   978-0-07-183759-0
MHID   0-07-183759-0

e-ISBN   978-0-07-183753-8
e-MHID   0-07-183753-1

Design by Mauna Eichner and Lee Fukui

Library of Congress Cataloging-in-Publication Data

Perruchet, Marie
  One perfect pitch : how to sell your idea, your product, your business—or yourself / Marie Perruchet.
 New York : McGraw-Hill, [2016] | Includes index.
   LCCN 2015042733| ISBN 9780071837590 (alk. paper) | ISBN 0071837590 (alk. paper)
   LCSH: Marketing. | Storytelling. | New products—Marketing. | New business enterprises. | Entrepreneurship.
   LCC HF5415 .P4364 2016 | DDC 658.85—dc23 LC record available at http://lccn.loc.gov/2015042733

McGraw-Hill Education books are available at special quantity discounts to use as premiums and sales promotions or for use in corporate training programs. To contact a representative, please visit the Contact Us pages at www.mhprofessional.com.

To those who helped me write my story
by letting me help them pitch theirs

CONTENTS

ACKNOWLEDGMENTS

···

First and foremost, thank you to my family for their inspiration and patience: my husband, Laurent, who supported me in my moments of procrastination; my six-year-old daughter, Evalouna, who exhibited patience far beyond her years; my parents, Jacqueline and Guy Perruchet, who nurtured my reading habits with fairy tales and encouraged my sense of adventure; Michèle and Yves Augis, and my grandparents, for always sharing good reads with me; my extended family in Normandy, Brittany, Paris, New York, and San Francisco, for their encouragement during the writing process; my public elementary school teachers, who taught me the fundamentals; Quentin Dickinson, who instilled in me the taste for true stories well told under pressure; and the media outlets that trusted me to tell stories to their audiences around the world.

This book would not exist without my McGraw-Hill editor, Casey Ebro, who first saw the potential in my writing a book about the perfect pitch and pitched the project to me.

I owe a big thank you to my development editor, Jill Rothenberg, who helped ensure that the book is as readable and engaging as possible.

A special thank you to Julien Cantegreil, for taking the time to review the manuscript carefully and to send me thoughtful feedback.

To Nancy Reyering, for her continuous encouragement since I settled in California; Stephane Meheux, for designing the One Perfect Pitch logo; and my friends from all over the world—from Belgium, China, England, France, Germany, India, Ireland, San Francisco Bay Area, Singapore, South Korea, Spain, Turkey—who often asked me how the book was coming along or congratulated me face-to-face, by e-mail, or by sending me cards I never replied to.

Thank you to all the entrepreneurial minds I came across, who have given me so much energy and happiness in my work.

I am also grateful to those who helped me get my book endorsed—thanks, Sumi Lim, Frederic Hanika, and Nicolas Genest, for your invaluable assistance—and to those who endorsed my book.

Thank you to the inspiring individuals I interviewed in the process of researching this book, including Kate

Albright Hanna, Zeinab Badawi, Gil Ben Artzy, Steven Cheng, Jeff Clavier, Gemma Craven, Kerry Dolan, Bob Donlon, Sean Jacobsohn, Nick Kanellis, Manana Mesropian, Marlon Nichols, Samantha O'Keefe, Keith Teare, Natacha Ruck, and Richard Zolezzi.

My heartfelt appreciation to all the experienced and first-time entrepreneurs whom I have met and will meet, who have the courage, curiosity, and commitment to work hard at improving their pitches and building incredible businesses.

And finally, to you, dear readers, who did me the favor of picking up the book at your local bookstore or clicking to buy it on your laptop, tablet, or smartphone. If what you find in these pages is useful, I hope you will share *One Perfect Pitch* with others so that more pitches can be improved and more stories of success told. Thank you.

ONE
PERFECT
PITCH

INTRODUCTION
Storytelling:
A Skill That Sells

....

In November 2008, I left my Radio France and BBC beats covering the turbulent changes in the world—from natural disasters to the skyrocketing business markets—to cover the Wild West of Silicon Valley. Those years overseas, crafting radio pieces on events ranging from the Kashmir earthquake in 2005 to the staggering growth of Shanghai as one of the world's new business capitals, helped me better understand the wide range of stories people tell to make sense of their world.

Whether it was reporting from Surat, the epicenter of diamond polishing, and learning about the lives of the workers who shaped the diamonds set on Mont Blanc pens that they could never afford or following the min-gong, the migrants who make up one-third of Shanghai's population, I listened to people's stories so that I could retell them to audiences who had never been to those remote places. Those years prepared me for my new role in Silicon Valley.

My goal was to help technology entrepreneurs create and tell stories about a new idea, a product, a business, or themselves that would appeal to their target audience.

At technology conferences in the Bay Area, what struck me immediately was the inability of startup founders to explain clearly and simply what they do. While listening to their presentations on demo days or during networking evenings, I saw that it didn't matter who they were—a Yale alum; a Stanford student; a recent MBA graduate; an Israeli, an Indian, a Korean, a Japanese, or a German entrepreneur; a very experienced CEO or a first-time business founder; a man or a woman—very few of them could tell an engaging and compelling story that would result in funding—and success. In other words, they could not craft a successful pitch.

Cultural differences don't matter. Regardless of your birthplace or background, you must hook your audience immediately by telling a story that is universal and that appeals to our collective human condition. The challenges faced by a Taiwanese entrepreneur pitching his startup in the food business, a Salt Lake City founder pitching her startup in the security industry, or an Italian entrepreneur pitching his solar car battery system are very similar. It's their ability to tell great stories about their businesses that will move an audience. Ultimately, it's the emotion that matters, not the language. This holds particularly true for many investors, who will tell start-ups' founders that ideas are less important than their execution by a brilliant mind. Cultural differences may not matter when you are hooking audiences, but learning the specifics of the successful Silicon Valley pitch is key.

All professionals, from fresh graduates to seasoned veterans, need to perfect their pitch. In Silicon Valley, we are in pitching mode 24/7.

Over the course of my consulting work, I became a mentor at 500 Startups, one of the most highly respected incubators in Silicon Valley. I use my experience in telling stories to advise startups on how to craft successful pitches. I design and teach storytelling and public speaking workshops and produce videos for technology companies in San Francisco, New York, and Europe, helping a wide range of smart, creative, hardworking, technology-savvy businesspeople to secure funding, to help clients better understand their work, to connect employees with management, or to recruit talent. But first, they must have a proper storytelling strategy. I help them figure out the very foundation of their story—their pitch.

My work led to the methodology you will find in this book. I provide strategies and tactics, as well as tips and exercises to help you craft your own pitch. These techniques can be used by anyone who is looking to improve his presentation skills and shape a new communication style that will win over his audience.

Storytelling is a skill that continues to gain popularity in the business world. Indeed, the ubiquitous question "What's your pitch?" has been replaced by "What's your story?"

In this book, you'll learn how to answer that question yourself—to simplify your storytelling approach, identify the important elements needed to engage an audience, understand what mistakes you are most likely making, and recognize how you can, by developing your storyteller's ear, correct them. Most important, you'll learn how to successfully sell an idea, a product, a business, or yourself.

EXERCISE
Your Story Audit

Let's get your story warmed up. By repeating your story, you become more adept at telling it and recognizing what resonates with the listener.

Think of up to 10 people with whom you have discussed your story over the past few months. You might have known them for a long time, or you might have just met them at a social gathering or on an airplane. Don't worry about the exact details.

List their names or initials here.

1. _____

2. _____

3. _____

4. _____

5. _____

6. _____

7. _____

8. _____

9. _____

10. _____

Based on their feedback, their reaction, and what you observed, the main strengths of my story as it exists today are:

(continued)

1. _____

2. _____

3. _____

The main weaknesses of my story as it exists today are:

1. _____

2. _____

3. _____

1

SINCERE
STORYTELLING

I work at the epicenter of global innovation, Silicon Valley, where stories of success and failure make the technology media headlines. After working with people from all walks of life and cultural backgrounds, I discovered that what I read in the fairy tales of my youth—the larger-than-life stories of ordinary people—contain the necessary ingredients of what I teach entrepreneurs today. A failed CEO in Silicon Valley, a rookie entrepreneur, a tsunami survivor—their stories follow a similar pattern: one of loss, struggle, failure, and transformation.

Every startup founder I know encountered hurdles and fought to surmount them. All of them almost ran out of funding and were about to shut down when an investor came through in the nick of time. Or their products were not selling, but after they changed the size of the packaging, their sales took off. Or they spent miserable days with their cofounders until they split up, giving their business a new direction. Despite bad times and against long odds, eventually, they got funding or their services were embraced by the market.

But you don't have to be a tech entrepreneur to know what it means to struggle. We've all experienced it—sometimes every single day. How we triumph over seemingly insurmountable obstacles and overcome is what gives storytelling its universal appeal.

We carry multiple stories that have shaped us—our childhood, our school years, our first loves, our families, our professional lives. Stories define us and shape who we are. And often our lowest moments—the periods of frustration, struggle, and, finally, turning points—are what help our stories take flight.

DEFINE THE STRUGGLE: WHAT BAD DAYS TEACH YOU

Stories are often about people having bad days—the very worst days of their lives—and struggling to get through them. Their experiences resonate with us because they remind us of very familiar situations, so we identify with them. They fight; we clench our fists. They fail; our hearts drop. They succeed; our pulses accelerate. We want to know what happens because we see ourselves in them. And perhaps what we learn will help us in the future.

Defining the struggle is a technique that I use with start-up entrepreneurs. First, show me the problem; second, show me how your product or service can solve that problem; and finally, state clearly why your target audience can't live without it.

Here is a sample pitch:

"Language learners' biggest barrier is the lack of opportunity to practice with native speakers. They learn Spanish or French at school, but they never become fluent. Or they learn on their own using a variety of resources, but they have no one with whom to practice. We have built a site where serious language learners can take tailored classes and engage in video chat with native speakers from the comfort of their homes. The online language learning market is worth $83 billion. Ninety-seven percent of the language market is still offline, so there is a tremendous opportunity and demand for our product."

This is better than saying, "We are a P2P video technology platform that provides tailored classes, etc.," which is not likely to captivate attention.

Illustrate these three points visually when creating a slide presentation:

1. The storm

2. The rainbow

3. The pot of gold

EXERCISE
Think of Your Doomsday Scenario

News outlets are often criticized for playing up bad news, but that practice is not surprising because bad news sells. When we hear a story, we want to know what has gone wrong rather than what has gone right, according to a study by the Pew Research Center in which nearly 200,000 adult Americans were asked about their interest in and reaction to some 1,300 news stories.[1]

For the scenarios that follow, focus on the details of how you solved the problematic situation.

- You had bills to pay, but you were low on funds. What did you do to get a new credit line?

- You had an important meeting to get to, but you were stuck at the airport with a missed connection. How did you get to your destination in time?

- Your business launched a product, and it tanked. What went wrong? How did you manage to sell the remaining stock?

- You opened a new office location. What problems did you face, and how did you solve them?

> How did these events affect you? How would you do things differently? And how do you tell these stories? Take a moment to write them down.
>
> Can you share them in just a few minutes? Time yourself.

VOUCH FOR THE CEO

It took Netflix seven years of tweaking to come up with the iconic red envelopes in which it mails rental DVDs to its customers. Netflix first used a heavy cardboard mailer. Then the company experimented with plastic envelopes, which were cheaper to produce but inflated en route. Then it went to a side-loading, micro-padded envelope with a bar code. You can imagine the team managers spending long evenings trying to figure out the best format to use, which probably made for some dramatic moments. These are the kinds of moments you want to focus on as you craft your story. Startup founders are disrupting old industries, and what they are trying to accomplish is changing how business is done. They are telling us a universal story of life, one of trial and error.

The hero's journey through periods of darkness to transformation is the foundation of many Hollywood movies and countless works of fiction and nonfiction. These periods go by different names in the startup world: high burnout rate, failure to get permits to operate, lawsuits, slow sales, buyouts, and, in some rare cases, IPOs (initial public offerings).

I work with clients who are competing with countless other startups for attention, users, partners, or money. Having a compelling story to tell is critical for success.

Many of these people struggle to explain what they want to build. Some recite a laundry list of features. Others are too detailed and use technical jargon that is unfamiliar to their audience, leading listeners to tune out. They need to learn how to structure a narrative into a relatable story that makes the problem and its resolution clear. We all know that a good story has conflict.

A question I often ask startup founders is, "How did you pick your company name?" At first, they reply, "We just found it," or, "We had a few beers and thought it was cool," or, "We put together a random string of letters playing Scrabble." But there is usually more to it: "We got sued by Belkin and had to change our name," or, "It's the combination of the three cofounders' names," or, "It means 'ear' in Japanese, and our device is for deaf people," or an especially good one: "It's named after Bruce Wayne's butler."

This question is a story starter. Very often, a startup's name tells much more about the company's story. For instance, if your software company delivers speed and performance in virtualized environments and its name is the Gaelic or Hindi or Latin word for 'lightning,' that's the backstory that people will remember. Or if most of your startup development happened during your commute on the L train or on flight 756, then tell that story.

> ### EXERCISE
> #### It's All in a Name
>
> What is the backstory you tell about your company name or brand? Did you brainstorm it? Did a branding agency do the work for you? Did you crowdsource it? How does it uniquely reflect your business?

FROM STORY TO PITCH

A story is at the heart of each conversation in Silicon Valley. Jeff Clavier, founder and managing partner of Soft-Tech VC, says, "My first question will often be, 'Hey, looking forward to hearing your story.' And I like the arc; I like a good story. A good story will mean that we'll listen to the pitch."[2]

What will make the difference between you and other storytellers is the format. The shorter your story is, the more interesting it will be. If you focus on the bare essentials and distill exactly what your business is, the problem it solves, and the transformation it promises, that's what will separate you from the others. A story in the entrepreneurial world needs to fit into a short format: 60 seconds, 5 minutes, or 10 minutes.

THE CULTURE OF STORYTELLING

What has become a much-sought-after skill has been around ever since *Homo sapiens* first gained the power of speech. Stories surround us. There are countless story times for children every week in public libraries across the country. Dozens of storytelling festivals happen every year, the largest being in Jonesborough, Tennessee, called the National Storytelling Festival. Radio shows such as *This American Life*, storytelling events such as the Moth, and oral history projects such as Story Corps are part of a large folk revival that is triggering interest among professionals from all industries who are using the narrative techniques in their daily business. "Storyteller" now appears as a title or an example of personal branding on

LinkedIn profiles or in job descriptions. In the end, we are all in the business of telling stories.

When we are schoolchildren, show-and-tell is one of the first ways we practice our storytelling skills. This is not so different from doing a product demonstration in Silicon Valley—except that in the latter case, the stakes are higher. It draws on the same skills. The audience may be more demanding than schoolchildren, but its members certainly share the same short attention span. The older we get and the more responsibilities we have, the more we forget what drives us to that stage in the first place: passion for what we are presenting and a desire to create meaning and excitement among the audience.

STARTUP STORYTELLING

Startup founders have never been in a better position to use storytelling to attract, convince, and win minds. And it works especially well for technology products. Technology companies are all about transformation. And storytelling is also all about transformation: characters face a challenge, they show us how they overcome it, and we see how they—and their products—change over time. That's exactly what technology companies are all about: transforming how we live every day, improving the way we eat, sleep, commute, communicate, and play. Technologies may be tools, but they shape the way we do things and therefore who we are. "Tech companies, in their many guises," says Intel company anthropologist Genevieve Bell, "always tell stories about the future of the world."[3]

Yet to convince investors of the value of their products, most startup founders and CEOs still rely on data-driven presentations rather than crafting a relatable story. A statistic, if it is not wrapped in a narrative, won't say much about a company, much less about the founder's journey and the resulting transformation. Lists of features and dry data are not how we remember. Stories are, because they give us the keys to understanding a changing world.

Munchery is a startup that prepares and delivers good healthy food that you can heat and eat in no more than 10 minutes. Its story illustrates well how one can align with a product.

Here is how Munchery's cofounders pitched their story.[4]

First cofounder:

Hi, my name is Tri, and I'm an immigrant. I'm one of those escaping boat people from Vietnam you might have heard about. When I was 11 years old, I escaped with my grandma and older brother in a tiny boat with a hundred people packed like sardines. We were in the open sea, under the hot tropical sun, for five days.

Despite the scorching heat, I will never forget how much water we had to live off of every day [meaning there wasn't enough water]. I eventually made it to an Indonesian refugee camp and was sponsored into the United States, but my parents never made it to the boat, so I didn't see them for another 11 years. After that life-and-death experience, startups don't seem that hard.

Second cofounder:

I've known Tri for over 10 years now. We first met at a Berkeley startup as early team members, where he ran engineering and I ran user experience. When Tri told me about the idea of Munchery, he was trying to solve a problem I knew very well. At the time, I had a 1-month-old and a 16-month-old, and it was really hard to plan for dinner. I didn't have much savings, and we both had really young kids. With the blessing of our wives, we both took a calculated risk and kissed our comfortable, high-paying day jobs good-bye to start Munchery. Failing wasn't really an option. Our families were on the line.

EXERCISE
Write Your Own Story

The Drama of Your Own Entrepreneurial Journey

- Did you have parents, a great-aunt, or a friend who showed you the ropes of entrepreneurship?

- Why are you so passionate about being an entrepreneur?

- How did you start?

- What was the breakthrough?

- How did you fight rejection?

- How did you find the first dollars to fund your venture?

Keep in mind that by telling the story of your entrepreneurial journey, you are beginning to craft your business story.

STORIES APPEAL TO UNIVERSAL HUMAN EXPERIENCE

No decisions are made, no products are sold, no partnerships are forged, no projects are approved, and no ships of state are launched based on a slide show of dry facts. Witness the powerful speeches that move hearts and minds: State of the Union addresses, inaugurals, nominations, eulogies, sermons, commencements, keynotes, and even locker room pep talks—they don't use PowerPoint. President Barack Obama's speech at the 2004 Democratic National Convention is a good example of how storytelling can both illustrate larger, often abstract political theory and appeal to universal human experience:

> And fellow Americans, Democrats, Republicans, Independents, I say to you tonight: we have more work to do—more work to do for the workers I met in Galesburg, Illinois, who are losing their union jobs at the Maytag plant that's moving to Mexico, and now are having to compete with their own children for jobs that pay seven bucks an hour; more to do for the father that I met who was losing his job and choking back the tears, wondering how he would pay $4,500 a month for the drugs his son needs

without the health benefits that he counted on; more to do for the young woman in East St. Louis, and thousands more like her, who has the grades, has the drive, has the will, but doesn't have the money to go to college. Now, don't get me wrong. The people I meet—in small towns and big cities, in diners and office parks—they don't expect government to solve all their problems. They know they have to work hard to get ahead, and they want to.[5]

Appealing to a universal human experience establishes immediate sympathy. All entrepreneurs think their product is unique. It is. It truly is. But it's their capacity to present this unique product as something that's universal that will resonate with those in the audience. It will make them think about their past experiences and friends who may share them. To create that for your audience requires sincerity and authenticity. You have to be real and vulnerable. That's how we remember you, your vision, and your cause.

What doesn't work is romanticizing your struggle, prettying up the real story, and obfuscating the truth. You want not only to be coherent and compelling but also to incorporate true elements with universal appeal in your story that your audience can relate to.

Sincere storytelling is how you capture our attention because that's how we remember and sympathize with your case, your cause, or your vision.

EXERCISE
Tell the (Ugly) Truth

Think about the hurdles you went through to find an apartment in San Francisco, or to get your license at the Department of Motor Vehicles, or to have your visa renewed.

What makes them uniquely yours?

- What was the conflict? What did you want that you couldn't get?

- How did the story end? How did you deal with the situation?

- Can you think of 10 people who have experienced a similar situation?

HOW STORIES AFFECT US

Psychological studies show that we aren't truly affected by a story unless we are emotionally transported, unless we lose ourselves in it. Paul Zak, professor of economics and the founding director of the Center for Neuroeconomics Studies at Claremont Graduate University, studies how this works in the brain. In one experiment, he paid research subjects $20 and then had them read a sad and compelling story about a father and his terminally ill son, taking blood samples from the subjects before and after they heard the story. At the end of the study, the subjects were given the opportunity to donate money to a charity for sick kids.

After the story, the subjects' blood samples showed spikes of oxytocin in the blood. Oxytocin has been called the empathy chemical. And the more oxytocin there was in the blood, the more these cash-strapped, empathy-drunk students donated to charity (on average, they donated half their pay). The study suggests what many of us probably already know, at least on a subconscious level: stories not only inspire us, making us feel sad, angry, or happy, but actually change our behavior by changing our brain chemistry.[6]

In another experiment, Professor Zak asked participants to watch 16 public service ads from the United Kingdom that were produced by various charities to persuade people not to drink and drive, text and drive, or use drugs. Participants were given either a synthetic oxytocin (in the nose, which reaches the brain in an hour) or a placebo. Those who were given synthetic oxytocin donated 56 percent more money than those who were given a placebo. Most important, these people said that they were less likely to engage in the dangerous behaviors shown in the ads. This experiment showed that when the brain is exposed to oxytocin, people are more likely to exhibit greater trustworthiness, generosity, charity, and compassion.

A study led by neuroscientist Gregory Berns, director of the Emory University Center for Neuropolicy, found that stories have a short-term effect on the brain. Most previous studies focused on the cognitive processes involved in reading stories while subjects are in the fMRI scanner. In contrast, the Emory study focused on the lingering neural effects of reading a fictional narrative. All of the subjects read the same novel, *Pompeii*, a 2003 thriller by Robert Harris that is based on the historical eruption of Mount Vesuvius in ancient Italy. "The story follows a protagonist, who is outside the city of Pompeii and notices steam and other strange things happening around the volcano," Berns says. "He tries to get back to Pompeii in time to save the woman he loves. Meanwhile, the volcano continues to bubble and nobody in the city recognizes the signs."[7]

The researchers chose the book because of its page-turning plot. "It depicts true events in a fictional and dramatic way," Berns says. "It was important to us that the book had a strong narrative line."

"The neural changes that we found associated with physical sensation and movement systems suggest that reading a novel can transport you into the body of the protagonist." Just thinking about running, for instance, can activate the neurons associated with the physical act of running. Berns says, "We already knew that good stories can put you in someone else's shoes in a figurative sense. Now we're seeing that something may also be happening biologically."

The neural changes were not just immediate reactions. They persisted the morning after the readings and for five days after the participants completed the novel.

BE REAL

The strength of our emotional response to listening to or watching another human being can change our behavior. That's exactly what startup founders are trying to accomplish by painting a new future. They invite us to step inside their worlds, showing us a new perspective or teaching us a new lesson or a new skill that we can celebrate together.

Just as fairy tales enable children to make sense of their world through an imaginary one, stories enable your audience to make sense of the choices you made as a founder, CEO, or entrepreneur. "The message that fairy tales get across to the child in manifold form is that a struggle against severe difficulties in life is unavoidable—is part of the human condition," wrote Bruno Bettelheim, therapist and author of *The Uses of Enchantment*, "but that if, instead of shying away, one steadfastly meets unexpected and often unjust hardships, one masters all obstacles in the end and emerges victorious. . . . Children through fairy tales identify with the hero in all his struggles and triumph with him when virtue is victorious. Adults follow a similar pattern of hero identification, who reveals truths about mankind and about himself."[8]

When startup founders share stories about what shaped their vision, it entices an audience to gather around them and act. For example, your target audience has a problem. Your role as a storyteller is to show the audience members how using your product will solve their problem and to motivate them to act on that information.

HOW STORIES ADD VALUE

There are common themes that appeal to audiences to help them sympathize and entice them to change their behavior. A fascinating experiment called the Significant Objects project was undertaken by *New York Times* journalists. In 2009, they invited several dozen authors to make up interesting stories about random objects that they picked up at thrift shops—a cat mug, an ashtray, a cow vase—and put up for sale on eBay. A Russian doll with a cloth mustache, originally bought for $3, sold for $193. A Utah snow globe bought for 99 cents sold for $59. A music box bought for 50 cents sold for $147.50. The authors spent a total of $128.74 on the items and made $3,612.51. The results tell us that stories add value to objects and that the value of an object increases once you learn the backstory. A lucky toy car given to the author by her brother after she failed her driving test three times but right before she took it for the fourth time, which was bought for nothing, sold for $41. Seventeen birthday candles found at the back of a drawer, sold for $21. A globe paperweight with a handwritten story about romantic escapades that was bought for $1.49 sold for $197.50.[9]

If stories add (measurable) value to objects, then sharing that value through a story is probably more effective than writing feature-focused ad copy or data sheets—and ultimately worth the effort. Stories strike an emotional chord, and sharing a personal moment that most of us can relate to makes for a universal story.

Sincere stories come from real and true moments in your life.

Next time you sell on eBay or Craigslist, Leboncoin, or Vestiaire Collective, think about the story you are going to tell.

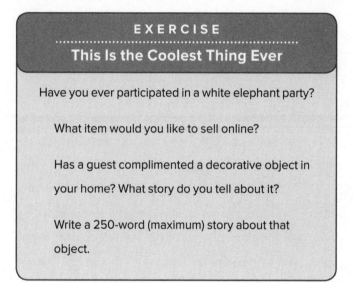

EXERCISE

This Is the Coolest Thing Ever

Have you ever participated in a white elephant party?

What item would you like to sell online?

Has a guest complimented a decorative object in your home? What story do you tell about it?

Write a 250-word (maximum) story about that object.

MINE THE STORIES OF YOUR PAST

Because entrepreneurs are so focused on the future, they tend not to look back on the past that shaped who they are today. Your early years as a founder are critical to shaping your core values. For example, I worked with an entrepreneur from Iceland who had created a fitness app. She had been a national judo champion in Iceland, so we were able to incorporate her lifelong passion for fitness as her motivation for creating a user-friendly app for the fitness buff. If you have created a language learning mobile application, then talk about your experience as a Russian military interpreter for the Israeli Special Forces.

When entrepreneurs weave past experiences and personal moments into a powerful narrative, it becomes a story that people want to hear. Sincere storytelling conveys your authentic self. Don't tell an overnight success story that no one believes.

Learning to tell your personal story is about taking what you already know and crafting it into a compelling and relatable story that will help you sell yourself, your cause, and your business.

STORYTELLING FOR ALL

What sets a storyteller and a startup founder apart is the format used to tell a story: the pitch. As we are moving toward shorter stories, entrepreneurs need to be able to explain what they do succinctly. They need to master the art of the perfect pitch.

Within companies large and small, the ability to tell a story that convincingly sells and promotes a product has become a sought-after skill. And corporations now think about the stories they tell their own employees to promote social cohesion, spur engagement, and enhance productivity. New employees may not know how the company started or the values that compelled the founders to create it. These origin stories need to be told within companies through personal stories that unify a group of people working together toward the same end. It is a great way to communicate the company's mission. How do you take the mission statement and translate it into personal stories that will motivate the troops? These stories should be retold internally and externally to establish and reinforce the solid foundation of the company and its brand story. This is true for startups and Fortune 500 companies alike.

Patagonia, the outdoor clothing company, featured customers' "reusing" stories in its "Worn Wear: True Stories of People and Their Patagonia Wear" advertising campaign. The company appealed to its customers' emotions, encouraging them to associate the "stories they wear" in pink fleece or down parkas with their memories of ski trips or weekend getaways. By doing so, Patagonia deepened its relationships with its customers. "This first fleece jacket hangs proudly on the wall at Patagonia

31

headquarters, but I had to take it down and try it on for old times' sake," said Patagonia founder Yves Chouinard, himself a good spokesmodel for the campaign.[10]

- Take professional photographs of your office. Show the light, the warmth of the office, and the people working at their desks. Take pictures of the outside, parking, and favorite hangouts nearby.

- Create a video in which the management and employees talk about how they first heard about the company, how they were introduced, and why they liked their first point of contact.

- Write a few blog posts about your mission, your customers, and your values.

GIFT YOUR AUDIENCE WITH YOUR STORIES

Over the course of my work, I have seen clients who don't realize the stories that live inside them until a professional— a trained storyteller, if you will—finds them and presents them. As a journalist, I uncovered bits that would exemplify how a person thinks to shed light on who he or she is. I use many of those same skills as a consultant, helping clients uncover what it is that makes them tick, what can be shaped into their stories.

I once coached a Scandinavian chef in his Brooklyn kitchen. He was preparing for an interview with the queen of Denmark and their team, who were in town looking for a chef. I was reading his seafood-inspired menu, and I observed his dual Japanese and Danish influences and his way of organizing the menu. After a few hours and many questions, everything fell into place. He had a fascinating story to tell about his early work in a Michelin restaurant, his fondness for fish growing up on an island, his stay in Shanghai, where the display of colors on the plate is a large component of traditional Chinese cuisine, how he was fired from the kitchen, and how he decided to return to the Japanese knife style of cutting fish.

The chef now had a story about his colorful path to this kitchen in Brooklyn, so far from both Scandinavia and China, one that spoke directly to how his wide range of influences made him both a traditional and an adventurous cook, grateful for his roots as well as for the foreign forces that shaped him. I'm pleased to report that he got the job!

People feel good and confident after they see the narrative of their life, a narrative that they can use and build on to advance their career or to promote their company. And good stories are not just relatable, they are inspirational.

They make us think; they make us feel. They stick in our minds and help us remember ideas and concepts in a way that numbers and text on a slide with a bar graph don't. Conveying the wrong turns, the losses, and the lessons turns a personal narrative into a universal story.

Stay close to your passion and who you are. This way, audiences will remember you. For corporations and startups, for founders and business leaders, for the professional who is looking to build a brand story, to communicate with clarity, to create relevant narratives, and to sell what's most important to you, here you will find proven techniques, examples, exercises, and—yes—stories to help you craft the perfect pitch. It's the transformative stories we tell that are truly magical.

I want you to see this for yourself.

EXERCISE
Escape Stories

Note: As you begin learning how to frame and distill your own story, you will want to build on it further by taking the time to explore it on paper. Think of this as a reporter would her notebook as she takes notes for a story. It's a low-tech but effective way to brainstorm ideas that will come into play as we take on the task of building your pitch. And once you've completed these assignments, you will have a handy reference that will help you build your future presentations.

Assignment:

1. Remember when you had to tell a compelling story to get out of an unpleasant situation. How did you tell it?

     Story prompts:

   - The police pulled you over. Which story did you tell—and brag about later—to avoid the fine?

   - It was a bad snow day, and commuting to work would be a challenge. You chose to stay home with the kids or catch up on Netflix. What did you tell your boss or your colleagues?

   - You traveled in a remote country, backpacking for a month. Which story did you bring home that gave you an Indiana Jones or Jane Goodall aura?

(continued)

2. Remember the last party you attended where you knew the host. Brainstorm three stories to tell other guests when they ask how you and the host know each other (met on a cruise, rescued from a fall on Mt. Tam, freshman college roommate). Get creative!

3. In each family, there is a storyteller.

   • Think of three stories in your family lore that come up every year.

   • How do you tell your favorite family story in which you are the star? Write down in 150 words a good story that gave you your nickname. How did it happen? Do your friends still talk about it? How does your family remember it? What made the nickname stick?

SUMMARY

For anyone who is looking to build a brand story, communicate with clarity, and create relevant narratives, storytelling can captivate the attention of large audiences and delight intimate audiences.

- Stories are about transformation: show this pivotal moment to your audience.

- Stories are about conflict: convey the relatable problem you are solving to those in your audience. Why should they care?

- Stories should be both authentic and universal: they should be drawn from your life but should resonate with your audience.

- Stories should be memorable: leave your audience members with a question, fact, or experience that they won't forget.

- Stories should be simple and succinct: make it easy for your audience to retell your story to others.

STORYTELLING RESOURCES

- Read and reread the classic fairy tales by the Brothers Grimm, Charles Perrault, and Hans Christian Andersen. You will find that they have lessons for today.

- Watch university commencement speeches at http://apps.npr.org/commencement/ to get a good sense of how speakers use stories to impart their messages.

- Read the transcripts of Nobel Prize acceptance speeches for more inspiration.[11]

BUILD
YOUR STORY

2

ONE PERFECT PITCH:
THE METHOD

As you know from crafting your own stories in the previous chapter, your job is to draw in your audience—to make its members care. In Silicon Valley, this is what entrepreneurs work hard to do day in and day out. Silicon Valley is one of the most competitive playing fields for anyone who is looking to start a business, drawing engineers, marketers, and other curious minds from all over the world who seek funding and customers. So how do you set yourself apart?

After years of working with a range of startup founders and entrepreneurs, I created an approach that would work for anyone who had a business idea or a product to sell. I call it the One Perfect Pitch Method. It works for entrepreneurs who are looking for funding, non-native English speakers setting foot in Silicon Valley for the first time, and CEOs who want to be more authentic and inspire their teams. It works for a 5-minute pitch, a 20-minute presentation, video scripts, customer stories, and keynotes. It works especially well in the tough world of Silicon Valley, where life is one big pitch.

In this method, there are three essential parts to creating your pitch:

- Flesh out your stories.

- Assemble your story in three acts.

- Make your presentation transformative (sign me up) or make the sale.

But first, here is what you can do to maximize your success before you get down to work:

- Start fresh in the morning or late at night when it is quiet.

- Switch off your phone—or set an alarm for every 90 minutes—to enable you to be at your most focused. Being in a place where there is no wireless connection would be ideal.

- Find a bright and quiet place. Wear a noise-canceling headset or earplugs if you cannot find a quiet spot. Face a garden, the ocean, or some other pleasing location. The view will relax your mind.

- Always have a notebook or Post-its to jot down notes.

- Give yourself a deadline (my hook in three hours; my customer case in three days). This helps you measure your progress and keeps you motivated.

- Take a break every hour. Even after a mere 10 minutes, you'll feel refreshed.

- Don't think you need to perfect your pitch or any part of it in your head before you start. As with all effective writing, your first draft will go through multiple revisions.

FLESH OUT YOUR STORIES

How do you win over an audience?

In a word: authenticity.

No matter who you are, whether you're an experienced CEO or a hopeful entrepreneur, there was a key moment when you decided to pursue your business idea, look for funding, and follow your dream. Whatever your goal, your mission is to communicate the passion you felt at that moment.

Your story is about the breakthrough moments that shaped who you are and what your product or company is. Those moments are true and will showcase your personality and your authenticity: your parents' decision to fund your engineering studies; the pen you used to sign the papers that started the company; how you filed the patent; a choice you made after an experience or person influenced you. Your job is to retrieve these moments.

When writing a pitch, think of identifying these breakthrough moments as analogous to looking under the carpet, where you might discover an old ring you thought you had lost, the missing piece of a giant puzzle, or a credit card that had disappeared from your wallet— all the pieces you need to convey the spark that drives you. My role is to guide you to lift the carpet because my experience has shown me that all the pieces are there.

For instance, a client renamed his company after its original name was repeatedly misspelled in the same way; he used the misspelled name instead. Another developed his product in Great Britain after British Telecom invited him to visit its campus. And still another wrote a new software program after he worked with government agencies as an IT contractor.

"A lot of founders get caught up in trying to follow a perfect template," says Sam Altman, president of Y Combinator. "Conveying your passion for the business is almost as important as what you say, and it's almost impossible to fake. Even if you're an introvert, it will usually come through to a sophisticated investor."[1]

Stories are powerful because they are true. Chances are that someone in your audience went through a similar moment or epiphany. That's how people will relate to you and remember you. But because the stories we are telling happened in the past, we often omit the details. We edit the story, forgetting that it needs conflict, turning points, and a resolution if it is to have lasting impact. Most of the founders I have worked with skip these moments, not realizing that it is precisely these moments that they should include in the stories they tell. "When people start talking about something they really care about, their passion is going to come through," says former CNBC journalist Kate Albright Hanna. Remember

EXERCISE
Breakthrough Moments

How did you decide on your last car purchase? Or your choice of a holiday destination? Or your last $100, $1,000, or $10,000 purchase? What arguments did you use to rationalize it? At what moment did you decide to vote for a particular political candidate?

Think about your high school or college years and the three friends you stay in touch with. Which memories about a particular teacher or class do you still recall and share? Which of these moments did you share with your classmates at the last school reunion?

those fundamental moments and use them to connect with your audience.[2]

There are three ways I help my clients get started: the picture approach, the emotive approach, and the draw a timeline approach.

The Picture Approach

When I listen to clients for the first time—telling me about their system network, their two-factor authentication, or their security system—I always create a drawing in my notebook because it helps me memorize what they do. Picturing a moment, a place, or a time helps you access your past. The more vivid the sensory details—sight, sound, smell—the more they will resonate with your audience. We retain images better than we do words, so re-creating a place, time, and action will help the audience relate more powerfully to what you do.

This is supported by science: a brain-imaging study by the Dynamic Cognition Laboratory at Washington University in St. Louis sheds light on what it means to get lost in a good book, suggesting that readers create vivid mental simulations of the sounds, sights, tastes, and movements described in a textual narrative while simultaneously activating brain regions used to process similar experiences in real life. "When we read a story and really understand it, we create a mental simulation of the events described by the story," says Jeffrey M. Zacks, co-author of the study and director of the laboratory.[3]

Associating images with situations or people is a good way to remember important information. So how do you make those associations stick? "Remember that the more particular the scene is, the more colorful your pitch will be," says Nick Kanellis of the Magnet Theater in New York City, where he teaches improvisation and works as a director with the Story Pirates. "You are painting a whole picture in your audience's head. So the more specific [you] are, the more they feel they are part of that reality."[4]

Details of the Location

You are pitching your industrial design skills. Remember the room where you designed your first prototype. Did it have carpeting? Victorian windows? You are pitching your team's expertise. Where did you meet? Were you at a Starbucks? Even Starbucks cafés are different. A leather sofa at the entrance gives quite a different feeling from a long wooden table. The more details you relate, the more accurate the picture and the more immersed in the reality your audience will be.

Time of Day

Remember the time of day when you decided to be an engineer. Was it evening or daytime? Was it warm, snowing, hot outside, or air-conditioned where you were? Revisiting those moments increases the number of circumstantial details and helps you recover even more memories.

What You Did Afterward

Do you remember where you celebrated the good news about your first beta version working? What did you do right after you hung up the phone with the investor who broke the good news to you?

The Emotive Approach

People frequently associate important events with strong emotions, so another good technique is to remember how you felt at a particular moment: after an announcement, after you received funding, after you decided to raise more money. These emotions will jog your memory; important moments will resurface. Communicating strong emotions in your story will help you connect with your audience and get your message across.

- During the early stage of building your product, when did you feel disappointed or pleasantly surprised?

- When did you feel exhausted or exceedingly joyful while working at that company?

- When did you feel anxious or confident about performing what you were told to do?

The Timeline Approach

Looking at events in your calendar may identify fundamental breakthroughs that will help you remember a story and enable it to emerge. Drawing a timeline gives you perspective on the development and evolution of your product. There's no such thing as an overnight success. "A success is rarely one little thing," says Elon Musk, CEO of Tesla Motors and cofounder of PayPal.

Draw a timeline (think of the history of your company or business) and consider these questions:

- When did you start working on the project?

- How did you feel on the day you decided to leave one company for another?

- How did you feel the moment you named your product or business?

- On the day you received news of your funding, what did you do to celebrate?

- What happened the day you created the prototype?

YOUR STORY IN THREE ACTS

Good pitches are succinct stories. They are fractals of your larger story. All this preparation is necessary to enable you to tell better stories that will let people connect with you. Once you flesh out your breakthrough moments, you need to simplify, organize, and structure your story for optimal audience recall.

"If you're constructing a way to present your story, you should be aware that most investors have short attention spans," shares Dave McClure, founder of the incubator 500 Startups. "They may be late to the meeting, they may be reading other stuff on their iPhones, so you want to organize your information in a way that allows them to process it more efficiently. . . . I'll be honest with you. Some days I'm just tired. My head is elsewhere. I need something structured like slides or a demo to orient me."[5]

Studies show that after a presentation, people retain only 10 percent of what has been said, and the percentage of what they will be able to tell others is even lower.

Your story is meant for the audience members to share. Make it easy for them to remember.

Structure and assemble your pitch in three acts. This will force you to think in a linear way that ensures that you cover all the bases of your pitch so that your audience can follow along easily. This also gives you a way to organize your thoughts.

"There's a huge cognitive comfort just in knowing you're on a story arc," says psychologist Pamela Rutledge, director of the Media Psychology Research Center. "We can tolerate the anxiety of the challenge because we know there will be a resolution."[6]

The three-act structure is similar to that of a play. You set the scene, the drama ensues, and the audience is pulled into the final denouement. Your presentation must both captivate and enlighten. You're on stage, and, in many ways, you're an entertainer—with a mission.

The Three Acts:

- Act I: Set the Stage (Tell me)
- Act II: Demo (Show me)
- Act III: The Transformation (Sign me up)

Act I: Set the Stage
(Tell Me/Hook the Investor)

Your opening is critical. A good opening triggers curiosity and promises investors a remarkable benefit. It draws them in, speaking to existing memories and experiences, and triggers an emotional response. Called a "hook" or a "teaser," it taps into stories, memories, beliefs, and values held by the audience. It's a signal to your audience to pay attention.

Very few speakers take advantage of this opportunity. I have heard many pitches begin with an apology or with filler words. Why waste those first few moments and not take the lead right away? You have only a few seconds to catch people's attention and persuade them to listen to you.

Think about this as the opening sequence of a James Bond movie. There is suspense; there is action; there is promise in the first five minutes that keep you glued to your seat for the next two hours. Grab your audience's attention from the very beginning. Otherwise, people will tune you out.

Brevity and catchiness are essential. Don't make people wait for the information. Your listeners have a limited attention span, so make the information digestible. Most people don't follow that rule, yet it applies to all sorts of pitches. During the first few seconds, those in your audience will form an impression of you and decide whether they will keep listening.

I often serve as a judge at pitch competitions where startup entrepreneurs pitch their ideas. I am always very attentive to how they walk onstage or "the first few silent seconds."

Here are some effective ways to lead with a bang:

1. *Silence.* Allow some silence before you begin. Savor the moment. Three seconds works well. However, waiting too long makes the audience uncomfortable.

2. *A gesture.* I advised a startup entrepreneur who had created a food delivery application to drop a Rolodex on the floor to illustrate the end of the Rolodex.

3. *A joke.* CNN anchor Anderson Cooper began his Tulane University commencement address with, "Does anyone else feel like you are at a Harry Potter convention? Either that or a renaissance fair?"[7]

4. *A statistic.* "Sadly, in the next 18 minutes when I do our chat, four Americans that are alive will be dead from the food that they eat," is how chef Jamie Oliver opened his TED talk.[8]

5. *A question.* "Did you know that 97 percent of the language market is still offline?"

6. *An ask.* "Your body language shapes who you are, so I want to start by offering you a free no-tech life

hack, and all it requires of you is this: that you change your posture for two minutes," is how HBS professor Amy Cuddy began her TED talk.[9]

7. *A shared experience.* "I grew up to study the brain because I have a brother who has been diagnosed with a brain disorder: schizophrenia. And as a sister and, later, as a scientist, I wanted to understand, why is it that I can take my dreams, I can connect them to my reality, and I can make my dreams come true?" was how Jill Bolte Taylor, neuroanatomist, opened her TED talk.[10]

8. *Common ground.* "It's very, very difficult to speak at the end of a conference like this, because everyone has spoken. Everything has been said," admitted Ngozi Okonjo-Iweala, economist and former finance minister of Nigeria, in her TED talk.[11]

9. *Kids or pets.* In his TED talk, Dan Pallota broke the ice with, "I want to talk about social inno-vation and social entrepreneurship. I happen to have triplets. They're little. They're five years old. Sometimes I tell people I have triplets. They say, 'Really? How many?' Here's a picture of the kids.

That's Sage and Annalisa and Rider. Now, I also happen to be gay. Being gay and fathering triplets is by far the most socially innovative, socially entrepreneurial thing I have ever done."[12]

10. *"Once upon a time."* Legal activist Lawrence Lessig started his TED talk with, "Once upon a time, there was a place called Lesterland. Now Lesterland looks a lot like the United States. Like the United States . . ."[13]

11. *The future.* "Thirty years from now, you won't be using your phone to make some calls."

12. *A confession.* "I need to make a confession at the outset here. A little over twenty years ago, I did something that I regret, something that I'm not particularly proud of, something that, in many ways, I wish no one would ever know, but here I feel kind of obliged to reveal," Daniel Pink admitted in his TED talk.[14]

Here's what's important to remember with your opening:

* You need to establish a common ground to bring the audience into your story and show that you share the same values. This lends you authority.

- Think about the audience first. You may be onstage, but the true star is the audience.

- Saying a few words in the local language—whether it's tech speak or a regional saying, if you find yourself in a different part of the country, for instance—can ignite your pitch.

Here are three effective hooks for your audience.

Hook 1: Talk About Momentum. Why Now?

Many people think that early-stage investment decisions are based primarily on reason and logic, when the reality is that emotion and momentum often play just as big a role.

Why are you pitching your project at this point in time? Explain the shift, breakthrough, or innovation that presented the opportunity to create a substantial new company. Talk about the size of the market because it will provide some perspective on your potential.

Here are some examples:

- There are 50 times more Internet users (2.4 billion).

- We all have one-click purchasing power (Apple, Google, Amazon, eBay).

- Sales at Asian fast food restaurants have grown by 135 percent since 1999, well outpacing the growth seen in any other segment, while global sales have increased by 482 percent in the same period.

A good way to think like the audience is to ask yourself what kind of breaking news its members will want to know. Talk about the structure of the market, the characteristics of your industry, the customer growth potential—these are important points that will fill in the background for someone who may not be familiar with your business. You want to do that work for your audience.

Here are some examples:

- A sudden cost reduction in the storage market

- More reliable access to the Internet

- Better smartphone cameras

- A new standard in the industry or a new compliance regulation

You want your story to be unique, but if you can't pinpoint at least a few anchors that validate your existence, you are going to have a hard time pitching it.

Pull research from a polling institute or from a reputable media publisher that has checked and sourced its numbers. Investors want to know what has changed in the world that makes this the perfect time for your company to thrive. Answering "Why now?" is definitely key to getting attention. But don't overwhelm people with a detailed analysis of the market. They want to be confident that you know what you're doing, but just show them the highlights.

Hook 2: State Your Achievements

One of the recurring mistakes I see with my clients is that they don't highlight their credentials from the very beginning. Don't bury the lead! Start with:

- We have been number one in the Apple Store in 26 countries for the past three months.

- In three months, we grew from a 150-square-foot office to a 3,500-square-foot building in the Flatiron area.

- We have received funding from Jeff Bezos, the founder of Amazon.

Starting your pitch with traction and showcasing your company's rapid growth, user acquisition, multiplied revenues, industry awards, or well-known angel investors as points of proof is a good way to get your audience's attention because it establishes your credibility and anchors the audience in what it is that you do.

Being upfront with metrics is an "expected dollars-and-cents attitude," notes Richard Zolezzi, a partner at the San Francisco law firm Nixon Peabody who brokers tech deals. Expressing yourself in terms of dollars may be uncomfortable, especially for non-Americans, but the audience you are pitching expects it.[15]

"Are you making any money yet?" George Kellerman, a former partner at 500 Startups, called out to a room of young Japanese entrepreneurs.[16]

Numbers matter. They signal that you know what you're talking about. Investors need to justify their investments to their company and to their general partners. They need metrics to help them do their job.

Opening your pitch by showing progress in your metrics will be exciting for your audience. That's your opportunity to link what you do to an anecdote and turn it into a powerful opening story that is universal.

Here are some things *not* to do when formulating your pitch.

Quote a Third Party's Interest
Never say, "Investors say they are interested in us," or "TechCrunch calls us one of the best startups they have

ever seen." Those statements don't make you look good, and they don't sound real. Instead say, "Our company's Series C round was led by the following investment firms. Ashton Kutcher and Mark Cuban were among those who invested." Or, "We ranked number 1 at the Apple Store in five countries five weeks in a row." This information is relevant.

Say Your Company Is Going to Be the Next Google

Such a declaration doesn't make a good impression because it doesn't sound credible. It undermines what you are going to say next.

Make It All About You

Count the number of "I"s in your presentation. It should be about those in your audience. What can your product, service, or business do for them?

Hook 3: Solve a Problem

All ideas originate from the observation of life: you were working on one thing, but something happened and led you to what you are doing now. Illustrating a problem is all about creativity, insight, and discovering a customer need. You are showing your audience how you came to work on the interesting idea that you decided to pursue. Are you solving a problem of your own that other people share? Did you discern a gap in the marketplace as a result of research? Did you observe a trend emerging? It doesn't need to be very long, but the audience needs to feel and understand the pain point. If you cannot convince those in your audience that something is broken, they will not be interested in a solution.

Too many entrepreneurs overwhelm their audience with the solution they offer and the technical and detailed features of their product or service but fail to explain the problem to begin with.

For instance, as a mentor for 500 Startups, I asked the teams to convince me why their products or services would be life-changing solutions.

Q: Why would I use your video editing service rather than the software I already use to edit videos recorded by my phone?

A: Because our service will enable you to edit your videos in real time, you will be able to post them on your blog three times faster, and you will spend less than one minute organizing them, which means that you'll free up space on your phone and have time to do something else.

Q: Why would I use your package shipping service rather than FedEx or UPS?

A: Because our service will save you the 20 minutes it takes to bring your package to UPS and will cost more than 30 percent less.

Entrepreneurs often focus too much on themselves rather than on the user, customer, or audience. Don't be that person.

For an investor to get excited about your idea, she needs to know that there is a big problem that cannot be solved by the existing solutions on the market.

Here are some examples:

- Millions of calls are dropped every day. Our company provides . . .

- Grocery shopping takes time away from other activities. Our app enables you to . . .

- Developers need app distribution, and consumers need a way to find apps that are relevant and timely. We provide website owners . . .

Know the people in your audience and offer simple solutions to their problems. Obviously, everybody faces different problems, so try to put yourself in your audience's shoes. Think about scenarios that will help you connect with its members most effectively.

For instance:

- Drivers searching for an open parking spot waste an average of x hours and x gallons of fuel every week and increase city traffic by x percent. Our company provides real-time data to . . .

- You want to hire the best engineers for your new venture. Finding the best talent for your team is a painful process. Our company matches talented developers with . . .

Airbnb is a good example of a service that we can all relate to and use. Airbnb's founders were struggling to pay their rent. There was a design conference in San Francisco, and the city's hotels were fully booked. They came up with the idea of renting out three airbeds on their living room floor and cooking breakfast for their guests. The next day, they created a website, airbedandbreakfast.com. Six days later, they had a 30-year-old Indian man, a 35-year-old woman from Boston, and a 45-year-old father of four from Utah sleeping on their floor. They charged each of them $80 a night. Airbnb is now worth $25 billion.

Why does this work so well? Explaining the problem you are solving helps you establish an emotional connection with those in your audience. Then they are ready to listen to the remedy. What's more, North American audiences respond very well to practical life situations.

Scientists and engineers respond even more strongly, as their industries are driven by the need to solve problems.

If you don't build an emotional connection through a real-life situation, people cannot visualize the problem and will not care about your solution.

Remember that connecting emotionally is good not only when you are pitching, but also at any time when you are speaking in front of an audience. Sharing a story or lesson from your own life always works well.

Here are some ideas to spark your creativity:

- Take your eyes off your screen and observe your surroundings.

  What do people do? How do they live? What are some of the obstacles and challenges they face as they go about their daily routines? This will help you generate ideas about the different problems your product or service will solve.

- Read about the topics of interest that are being covered in the pages of the local newspaper.

- Ask people how they would use your product differently and what solutions they can offer.

Listen carefully. You'll be surprised at the answers, which will show you how differently people see things.

EXERCISE
Frame Your Hook

Fill in the following:

We solve [problem] by providing [advantage], to help [target] accomplish [target's goal]. We make money by charging [customers] to get [benefits].

We are [credentials], and this is how we got to our [insight]. This is why we're good at doing this. And from this insight, we can make you [amount of money].

Or:

I've always been curious as to why, in this market, it seems that all these companies are doing it [this way]—but it's not working. We decided [our way] is better. And it's actually working.

Why Is the Hook So Important?

When you're addressing an audience for a short amount of time, you immediately need to establish a bond and show your listeners that you share the same values. A hook that speaks to breaking news, information that is relevant to them, or a problem that they face increases the perceived value of what you are going to say.

"You want the person you're pitching to become part of the story that you're telling," says Natacha Ruck of the Stanford Storytelling Project. "If you can give them that arc that makes them part of the story, then they will be convinced."[17]

It also gives your investor a good sense of what the situation is. A strong hook allows your listeners to see the world you envision and the transformation that needs to take place for it to become a reality.

Act II: Demo (Show Me)

To show that your product or service is superior to the competition, you need to do a demonstration. It can happen in a small meeting room in front of an investor, it can be in a noisy hall at a 20,000-attendee conference, or it can be on stage in front of 2,000 people. In all cases, you need to be prepared. And based on my experience, you are never prepared enough.

One of the recurring mistakes that entrepreneurs and technical teams make is that they don't think in terms of value for their users, customers, or partners. They enumerate a boring, repetitive, and comprehensive list of 20 untailored benefits. Instead, they should think in terms of what will compel the audience to choose their product, their business, or their skills over all the other sexy alternatives on the market—alternatives that include doing it themselves, having partners do it, and doing nothing.

What will make people drive across town in city traffic to get to you? What will make people line up and camp out for 24 hours before the opening of the shop to get the new release of your product? What will make them tell their friends, their families, their boss, and their board that what you've created is so exceptional? What will make people think that what you have is worth investing in?

"Just because," "because I need money," or "because you happen to be a friend of my friend" is not enough these days. You have to prove that you are the only one who can do the job.

Here are some of the most common mistakes. Avoid them:

- "I love my product."

    Don't assume that it will be evident to people that your product is great and that they will love it as much as you love it. What is it that your product can do for your clients? What benefits does it provide? What's in it for them? Why should they care?

- "My product has a list of 50 killer features and functions."

  Do not communicate too much information. You can't do that during the pitch because people won't remember everything about your product. This is a very common error made by foreign-born entrepreneurs who are unable to communicate the value of what they do. Think clearly about what separates you from your competitors in a particular field. Focus on three key differentiators. There is no need to overwhelm people with a list of 50 points that will dilute your message about what makes your product or service so great.

- "My product is easy to use."

  This is probably the least imaginative approach—and the most common. Use precise words. Don't use the words *better*, *faster*, and *cheaper*, because they aren't precise enough. Besides, that's what most of Silicon Valley is trying to do. A key differentiator should be specific. All customers expect good value, fair prices, excellent customer service, and reliability, to name a few. You are bringing unique value to your market. You solve a unique problem for your customers. That's the key differentiator.

Here are some tips on how to come up with and fine-tune your key differentiators:

- Think about the most authoritative feature or function that you can measure or quantify. What makes your product unique? A patent. The one that no one else has. It works across all platforms. It has secure data encryption developed by the first Google engineer. What is the technological advantage?

- Remember the last time a client, user, or partner told you about your product's efficiency. What did the person say?

- Remember your last interaction with a client who loves your product. What made him rave about it? What makes your product or service superior?

- Remember the last time you said you had an A team. Who is the human resource who stands out and affects your product the most? Who is the Facebook cofounder on your team?

- What part of the market do you own, and what makes it unique?

- What is your point-of-sale advantage or distribution method? Do you need to go to the store to buy it? Can you do it online?

Knowing and articulating what sets you apart and weaving it into a good story about what your product does or the future your product promises will help your audience understand who you are. It will also help you recruit the best team members, who are aligned around those values and will create your company culture.

These techniques also work when what you are selling is yourself. I worked with a client in Silicon Valley who was a graduate of Stanford University, had done stints at Facebook and Google, and was looking to change companies. Many other candidates in a 50-mile radius had a similar profile. But no one matched who she was by 100 percent. How do you tell a better story about yourself?

We qualified and quantified her achievements: her participation and involvement in the Stanford community, the percentage increase in annual memberships she was responsible for at a previous company, the team leader role she had played to improve efficiency at Facebook, and her passion for social issues. That's how she was able to stand out.

Another great way to show that your product is superior is to quantify it.

Here are some examples:

* By using our product, physicians improved their per-visit margins by five times. The care

of a patient from diagnosis to treatment now takes less than 2 minutes, compared with the 20-minute average for office visits.

- Our solution enables you to cut the cost of transport by 80 percent.

Listening to your users, observing how your team members react and what drives them to speak with such passion and energy about your product, and asking for feedback from people who are not specialists are good ways to gather information about what makes you, your product, or your service so unique.

EXERCISE
Out the Window

Studies show that to engage those in the audience, you have to stimulate their senses. Stimulate your listeners with an odor, a tactile feeling, a sound, or a taste. Use vivid, concrete, sensory details to paint a more complete picture.

Take a few seconds to look out the window. What do you see? Describe as many details as you can see, hear, or smell.

EXERCISE
Tell Sensory Stories

Touch

You have built an educational smartwatch to track kids' progress. How does your device feel?

cool—slippery—fragile—furry—satiny—velvety—
elastic—leathery

Finding the right word determines the stickiness of the story.

Example: "Unlike other smartphone technologies, our smartwatch is designed with children in mind. It has a nonslippery band and a furry design that delights kids."

Taste

You have developed a healthier yogurt. How does it taste?

tart—sweet—fruity—gingery—medicinal—buttery—
minty—salty—peppery—bittersweet

Example: "I have always loved yogurt—the thick kind I grew up eating on the banks of the Bosphorus in Turkey, where my mother made it from scratch on our family's dairy farm. When I moved to the United States, I found yogurts to be too sugary and watery. I saw an ad featuring a fully equipped yogurt factory for sale: Kraft owned the yogurt factory and decided that it wanted out of the yogurt business. That's how Chobani yogurt started."[18]

Smell

Of all the senses, that of smell is the most strongly connected to memory. What if your TVs were equipped with olfactory cartridges that could release scents? What smell would you like to have in your living room?

sweet—fresh—fruity—minty—crisp—clean—lemony

Example: "Savor the clean scent of lavender while watching an ad for a new detergent. Breathe in the aroma of Colombian coffee during George Clooney's Nespresso commercial."

Sound

You don't necessarily need to have a digital music streaming service to animate the story of your product

(continued)

with sound. Perhaps you've found a solution to cancel outside noise and listen to your desired music without wearing a noise-canceling headset. Or you've designed a motorbike racing engine. What would it sound like?

hum—peep—whistle—tumult—loud—mutter—
mute—roar—whine—rumble—faint—squawk—
jangle—hiss—thunder

Example: "Traditional home security doesn't work. False alarms disturb neighbors and are often ignored by the police. Our smart home device technology detects unusual activity and alerts you with a customizable alarm."

Your Product in Action

When pitching to an investor, get to the demo as quickly as possible. If you have built an application or a platform or if you have a prototype to show, this is the time to show it. If you have set the scene properly, the audience will be eager to see it. Just as comedians, actors, and other performers use props, you will use your demo to enlighten, educate, entertain, and, most important, sell to them.

The Rule of Three

Enumerating a progression of three builds up tension before a release. It's an effective technique to enhance recall. Three has been used to convey memorable concepts, ideas, names, and brands.

- Literature: the Three Musketeers, the three little pigs, Aladdin and his three wishes

- Cinema: the good, the bad, and the ugly; the original Star Wars trilogy

- Slogans: Yes, we can; Just do it; veni, vidi, vici

- Sports: gold, silver, and bronze medals; triathlon

- Companies: Bed Bath & Beyond, IBM, CNN, CBS, BBC, UPS

- Theology: the Trinity, the three wise men

Keep in mind that the demo should support what you have just said. It's a continuation of the story you started with the problem. If you said that your product is simple to use, it should exhibit that simplicity. It should support and reinforce the benefits of the solution you have just shared with the audience.

The investors shouldn't be thinking about anything else when you are walking them through the demo. The flow from the hook to the demo shouldn't be interrupted because you are changing the scenery—it's part of the same story. If you have nothing to show, tell a customer story.

Zappos, the online retailing website, features snippets of employees doing a video demo of its products. Zappos reported that these videos increased its leads by 33 percent.

When should you include the demo? It depends on how much time you have. It is important that the demonstration show the technology that is powering your business. Your audience may not be as knowledgeable about technology as you are. Remember that experiencing a live demo is far more engaging than listening to a founder who is showing slides.

The demo should come after you've wowed them with your hook. It should highlight the benefits that your product delivers for a specific user with whom the audience can identify. It doesn't explain how you created the app or how difficult it was to find a developer. It shows your intention and the product's purpose. "Customer x is looking to do x. Let's walk you through how she would do that using our x solution."

One of my clients had an online booking platform for video classes. I suggested he start his demo by talking about Peter, a guitarist from the Czech Republic who was hoping to grow his fan base by giving guitar lessons. He showed us how Peter had an online calendar that was searchable on the platform. Fans or students would click on his calendar to book a session with him and pay through the platform. During the demo, it was important to highlight the easy booking and transactions features of the platform. After his presentation, the investor was confident of his capability.

A demo gives audiences the opportunity to see your product in action and how you interact with it.

Unfortunately, there are many ways to mess up a demo, in addition to the external factors that you can't control (a fire alarm, cell phones ringing, and so on). Too many presenters mistake a demo for a reading and it is not that. It's more like a show-and-tell on steroids. Many entrepreneurs also believe that a demo, the act of showing the audience what you are offering or selling, stands by itself. They can't keep their demo under 15 minutes. "I don't need to practice because I know my product so well," is something that I have heard many times.

As with any piece of a presentation, a demo needs structure and dramatization. It is a story, after all. It requires practice and rehearsal. You need to assume that something will go wrong: the network connection will fail; you'll trip on stage; your tablet will crash; the lights will flicker; you'll forget your computer. You need to be extremely prepared to speak without a demo and leave your audience with the same message.

Here's some advice on how to set your story in action.

Be Consistent in Your Storytelling

Example: "We helped Customer x from Company x do x with our product. Let us show you how."

Your demo should match and reinforce all the key differentiators that you highlighted before and should be woven into a structured story. Think of your demo as a "controlled narrative" of your product, exposing only what those in the audience need if they are to get on board, whether they are in the same room or far away. It's important to be consistent so that you can touch on the points you brought up before.

For instance, suppose the product is a toy equipped with a voice recording message system for kids who miss their parents when they are away.

"It's bedtime, and the child is crying because she misses her mom. Here comes the plush toy. It's warm, fuzzy, and cozy. The child takes the plush toy, looks at the belly, clicks on the felt belly button, and listens to the recorded message from her mom. The recorded message is of better quality than any voicemail. What did Mom do during the day in between her meetings? She opened the app, clicked on the red button, and recorded her message, which was directly uploaded to the platform linked to the chip embedded in the toy, which plays the message."

We don't need to know that the platform can record multiple voice users and hosts 2 GB of data, that the child can't accidentally erase the message, and that the recording is not going to play unless it's activated. All we need to know is that it is safely embedded in the toy's stomach, that it's a one-button voice recording of the parent triggered by the child, and that it doesn't sound like a robotic voice—as other plush toys do.

Present a Day in the Life of a Customer

If you don't have the product to show, tell a customer story. Create an imaginary character. Walk us through his painful day. Show him experiencing real problems that are solved by your (new) product features. Enliven the character with characteristics similar to those of the audience, so that we can see the world through his eyes. Remember that his day should be organized in a logical way, step by step, so that the audience can follow along and wonder what's coming next. The customer story should take the audience on a journey of discovery about why your product or service is worthy and necessary. This is the crux.

- Perform the actions one has to do in order to use your product: "Click here to open the app. This is what you'll see. Do this. Here is the result. Pull that. Here is what happens."

- Performing actions is the best way to paint memorable pictures in the mind of the audience.

- Keep it short: no more than a dozen performed actions so as not to overwhelm your audience. Think in terms of an action-result perspective: What does each action do for the user?

- You can show your demo or tell your business customer case for anywhere from 40 seconds to a few minutes. Do not go for more than 10 minutes. You will lose people's attention.

I sometimes have my clients start their pitches by telling business case stories because they offer real-world examples that help their audiences understand what they do in a nutshell. For example, I worked with a top executive of a software company who had to talk about the value of his enterprise storage solution on camera. I asked him, according to client feedback, what his customers liked most about his solution. Not what was on the list of features but what they said in their own words. He told me about a corporate client who was experiencing slow connectivity between the Austin office and the Raleigh office, which forced teams to wait for file access. Using his service reduced the client's file storage costs by 40 percent and increased team productivity by 20 percent.

Think About the Timing Within Your Presentation.

The shorter, the better. Don't get lost in your demo. Time it so that it's 10 to 20 percent of your presentation. For a 1-minute pitch, make it 10 seconds. For a 20-minute presentation, keep it under 2 minutes. For an hour-long presentation, keep it to 10 minutes. Running out of time and not conveying the entirety of your message can hurt you.

Keep It Simple

"Hide the complexity; expose the simplicity," a chief technology officer in the Bay Area once told me. Computer science is all about abstractions, after all. Make it simple to understand. If you complicate it unnecessarily, this can signal to investors that you don't know what you are talking about. A complex idea can be explained in a simple manner. Because you have a limited amount of time, use clear, concise, and easy-to-understand language and avoid buzzwords or jargon, which can turn people off.

Be Prepared to Pitch Anywhere, Anytime

Does your demo rely on Wi-Fi? This generally is not a good idea because you may not have access to it, or your remote access may not work. Make sure you have a demo that can be done in the most unusual situations, such as underground in a subway car or in a noisy bar or restaurant. You are in 24/7 demo mode in Silicon Valley. If you're presenting on screen, make sure to close all other programs. You don't want your iTunes library visible or to have photos of your family pop up when you're about to make your pitch.

The Intern Shouldn't Be Doing the Demo

Who is doing the demo? Is it the CEO? The VP of engineering? Who is managing the slide transitions, the push-of-the-button transitions? Is it a one-person show? Even if one person on the team is clearly the best presenter, if you're on stage, you should say something. It's awkward to have someone just stand there. Split the work, if possible. Have the CEO talk and another person work on the cues. If the same person does both, she may look at the screen too much and worry about managing the transitions instead of being present while doing the demo.

Do Some Research Before the Meeting

Think about the room. It's always good to make sure you have enough space to do the demo. Always stand on the right side of the screen when you're on stage or using your iPad to do a PowerPoint or Keynote demonstration. Eyes travel from left to right. Do you have enough space to move around and marshal your thoughts? Don't stand behind a podium. It's always worth it to do a dry run, if possible. In the same room, rehearse an hour before in order to be as close as possible to the actual presentation. If you have to adjust the sound button for the video, you may want to prep with the technicians.

Act III: The Transformation (Sign Me Up) or Making the Sale

By now, you should have the audience in your pocket. With all of the necessary focus on pitching and telling your unique story, you don't want to omit one of the most important details: how you make money!

The third act is where you dive into the more financial aspects of your product or business and how you will execute with your team. Make sure that you have projected into the future.

All entrepreneurs face the same challenging task when looking to explain their business model: keep it simple.

Focus Your Business Model

The idea is to show how much of the market you are going to address and capture and how you will generate revenue. Presenting too many sources of funding is confusing to your audience and shows a lack of focus. Prioritize one and keep the others as ideas to develop further. You may explain the first one well, but when you get to the second one, investors may start wondering what was wrong with the first one. And by the time you get to the third one, they may not be listening anymore.

Samantha O'Keefe, the TechCrunch Disrupt editor, says, "Early-stage companies are still figuring out their product market fit and how they're going to monetize, who their first customer is, and so on. I see teams telling me the three different revenue streams they have, which is very confusing to communicate in a short period, and also doesn't give the people listening a lot of confidence that the team is really focused and headed in a specific direction."[19]

Dave McClure, the founder of 500 Startups, agrees. "The business model is AKA how do you make money.

I am a big fan of simple revenue models, typically direct models, either transactional or subscription. When you're listing sources of revenue, I recommend that you keep it simple and keep it to one or two. When you list a large number of sources, that tells me that you don't know how you're making money."[20]

While Dave McClure acknowledges that some investors may have a different point of view, "listing five or ten sources demonstrates a lack of clear focus on where the bucks will come from. If you do have a bigger list, at least prioritize them by biggest first," he added.

If you make it too complex for investors, it will be even harder to explain to customers. Focus. Don't try to dazzle your audience with too many numbers. It will backfire.

Research Your Competitors

I often hear the following from clients looking to pitch their product or service: "We have no competitors." Um, no. That's probably not the case. You need to either spend some time doing research or pay a research person or institute to do it for you. This will help you understand your key differentiators and refine your position in the marketplace.

While I was doing some research for one of my clients, I found a competitor who was from the same country and who had created a similar app with a similar goal. Knowing the competition enabled us to prepare well. We were able to take a different tack on the product and the brand story.

If you don't do your homework, chances are that your user or your customer will discover your competition or that you will eventually find yourself in front of an investor who may have already considered or even invested in your competitor. You will lose credibility if you didn't do your research, are ignorant of the marketplace, and are unable to convince your listeners to invest in you instead of in your competition. Knowing your competitors means that you can articulate their weak points and state the ways in which you are different.

You may have fewer than five competitors now, but you may have other nascent competitors in other countries who will be coming after you on your own turf. Being aware of this shows that you know what you are doing and that you have confidence in your product.

As a business owner and as an entrepreneur, you always want to be ahead. Knowing what your competitors are up to is a survival skill.

Show Your Expertise

Many of the CEOs I have worked with are experts at explaining their job transitions, major career pivots, and school-to-career paths, but most of them underestimate the value of telling their full story as part of what they are selling. "The secret sauce is in the entrepreneur," says Barbara Corcoran, one of the "sharks" on *Shark Tank*. "We have education on how to write a great business plan. They go get their fancy Harvard MBA, they get all the fancy terms down, they feel capable; it's a misnomer. What's very hard to teach in schools is personality. How do you change somebody's personality and make him the kind of person who is going to succeed in business? You can't teach personality, it's a hard thing. . . . The number one thing is, how well do you take a hit? You must have a low IQ to get hit, go down, pop back up, and say, 'Hey, I am down; hit me again.' But you know, those are the entrepreneurs that will succeed, who will find a way to get to the finish line. They know how to get the ball forward."[21]

Of all the startups that are as competitive as yours, why is yours more likely to succeed? Telling a story about your team is one of my favorite parts of coaching entrepreneurs, because that is when I grasp the layers and the depth behind what makes an entrepreneur: what drives her, what makes her wake up every morning, work very long hours, and still have faith in what she does.

One morning, you have an investor who shows interest and is about to sign a check. The same afternoon, you lose a business account. The following day, you hear nothing from the investor. Nor the week after. Then suddenly another investor shows up and pays attention. The same hour, you are bringing 1,000 users onboard and your system crashes. Or you have been working for the past four years, burning your investors' or your own money (or the bank's or the government's money), and you haven't generated any revenue. Yet you are the talk of the town. What keeps you going when everything is hurting—when you are on the verge of quitting, when you see yourself crashing and burning, yet you hold on, you persist?

Recall the most important and lasting influences on your life thus far. How can you use them as the foundation of your narrative, to illustrate what really drives you? How do stories tucked away in family albums help explain why you do what you do? How do you show that you are a man or woman who is worth investing in? It's not a class you take or a framed diploma on your wall. It's how you relate what matters to you in story form.

- Childhood

  Example: I have been obsessed with Asian cuisine since I was a kid. My parents literally made fun of how much Asian food I ate. It's no surprise that I created an Asian food delivery service.

- Family

     Example: My dad used to work as a power line engineer. He talked about grid power losses at the dinner table. Last year, 1.2 trillion metric tons of CO_2 were released into the atmosphere. I created a technology that can eliminate that loss in the future.

In a competitive marketplace of ideas, your story needs to show how and why you are the best at executing what you promise. In short, give me some evidence of your expertise.

If you have performed a task, taken an action, or built a product 20 times with the same outcome, say so. Serial entrepreneur. VP of product development at three companies. If you have not done it 20 times before, you have to find parallel experiences that demonstrate that you can do it. What other situations in your personal or professional life reflect that tenacity to succeed? The irony of a beautiful story is that it doesn't come from the rosy side of life. Change and transformation come from the dark side of things, from what makes us struggle, what makes us suffer. Think about problems you faced in the past in your former companies and what actions you took that led to success. Tell your investors how you responded to an unexpected situation. What have you accomplished that best exemplifies that you know to get things done?

> ### EXERCISE
> #### Breakthrough Moments in Your History
>
> What were your interests and skills in your early years? How did you spend your time before you were inundated with work e-mails, bills, and problems? Rediscover your interests and unearth your predispositions. How can you relate those answers to the work you pursue today?
>
> What were some of the most extraordinary situations during your childhood when you felt a sense of accomplishment? Which moments do you remember that made you the talk of the class?
>
> If you've volunteered, what was the most rewarding experience? The most difficult?
>
> How did you feel when you coded, or learned some other new skill, for the first time?

Think about what drives you. What brought you to this moment when you are trying to secure funding for your business, product, or service? It's a calling—not a job. As journalist Katie Couric said in her commencement speech to Trinity College in Hartford, Connecticut: "I knew I had to be a journalist because I am deeply curious about the world, I love to write, and I saw that when properly practiced, it's a craft that can help galvanize an often complacent citizenry, and make a difference."[22]

Demonstrate the Expertise of Your Team

You need investors to protect you from any contingency that will keep you from developing, building, and achieving what you promised you would do, but still lose their money. To convince investors that you and your co-founders are not going to part ways, go to war, or simply quit, showing that your marriage is solid and is going to work also conveys strength in your product.

You want to show the bond that glued you together in the first place: What makes you partners in crime? You were childhood friends. You were college roommates. You worked on the same team at the same company for five years. Some teams are built over beers in a bar.

How does an investor know that you are not going to run away with his check, or spend it on lavish five-star hotels, get massages all day, and not develop what you promised? Investors want to know that entrepreneurs have what it takes to run a company and give them an exceptional return on investment.

Show Your Confidence

Show a history of success that clearly communicates your personal achievements at your company. When did you know that you could do it?

Confidence comes from knowing your product, your research, and your user.

Get rid of "unconfident" words. Using "I think" or "I'll try" implies indecision and uncertainty. Tell people what you are doing, not what you are trying to do. If you currently are not doing it, say how you are going to execute, build, or develop it. Too often, people interject these simple words that can detract from the force of their presentations. "Our product is" sounds more authoritative than "I think." You need to show that *you* are the expert.

As a mentor at 500 Startups, giving feedback to hundreds of teams, I have learned that there is a fine line between showing competence and being overconfident. Sticking to the facts and giving accurate information prevents self-promotion and generates trust. "All of the evidence from psychological research suggests that humility makes you more likable, even in the U.S.," says Tomas Chamorro Premuzic, professor of business psychology at University College London. "So that is when people perceive that you are more competent than you think you are, they will like you more. And conversely, when they see that you are less competent than you think you are, they will like you less."[23]

Tell the Truth

Stick to the truth. It is much easier to build on real-life situations than to invent new ones that will unravel under scrutiny.

Audiences are smart and can easily detect what is fake. There is no reason to inflate or transform the truth. That's what most of the investors I spoke with insisted on. I asked Ben Horowitz, general partner of the Silicon Valley firm Andreessen Horowitz, what his best advice was for entrepreneurs when pitching. He wrote, "Marie, always tell the truth."

The truth is about the main character in the story: you.

Focus on the Positive

When you are sharing your story, give your audience a sense of what your life looked like before you decided to move forward with your venture. I went through this myself. I had been a journalist. I covered politics, not technology. Storytelling was starting to make the enterprise headlines, and the startup CEOs I worked with needed help in pitching and telling good stories. The need was so great that it pushed me to start One Perfect Pitch. That's where the business need was, so I made the transition from journalist to pitch coach and communication consultant. I haven't looked back since.

Don't Forget Your Ask

I have listened to countless pitches that leave the audience with nothing to do. The pitch doesn't have an ask.

In my work with clients, I advise speakers to give a clear sign that the story is coming to an end. Stories are about character building and character transformation. They're about personal development. All good stories—and pitches—have an ending.

Many times, presenters leave the audience confused. As crucial as the hook is for captivating those in your audience in the first few seconds and having them listen to your whole story, a strong ending will keep your listeners' minds on your ask. What it is that you want from them? A second meeting? An introduction? Funding? A job? Approval for a business plan? Do not leave your audience in the dark. If you are presenting on-stage, circle back and refer to your hook to provide a sense of closure. Repeat the key sentence of the presentation. Make a call to action: Sign up. Visit our booth. Introduce us.

When you are writing your pitch, you need to start with your vision and end with what you want your audience to do for you. Remember that you are selling your vision of the future, and you want your audience to be part of the story that starts as soon as you stop pitching.

You took the stage. You connected with your audience. You left people with an ask and something to ponder.

Now you are ready to do it again—and again.

EXERCISE
Spotlight the Drama

This exercise will get you thinking about different ways to approach your business—your brand—from different angles.

If you could personify your brand, your product, or your business, what attributes would you give your character? What would be his or her abilities? What would you have him or her represent for people that would let them immediately understand your business? Try to keep it to 250 words.

EXERCISE

It's All in the Details

When you started building your product, what TV shows were you following?

- The last time you had to present in front of the executive team, what outfit did you wear? Do you remember how you wanted to project yourself that day?

- The last time you heard bad news about your business, what did you do afterward?

Using the following terms, pick three combinations to show how you felt about your professional experience, your product development, or your business performance.

Proud/Embarrassed

Courageous/Timid

Accepted/Rejected

Despondent/Excited

Amused/Shocked

Jealous/Happy

Worried/Hopeful

Respected/Unappreciated

Relaxed/Stressed

Fearful/Joyous

Nervous/Elated

Frustrated/Honored

EXERCISE
For an Investor's Pitch

How did you come up with the idea for your business? What was the day like? How did you feel? What motivated you to act on your idea?

Formulate it in 150 words, according to this template:

I observed . . .

then I thought . . .

but it didn't work well because . . .

then I did . . .

and finally . . .

Memorize Your Story

Feel the story in your bones. Through movement, get the feel of the material. Close your eyes and visualize the action. This often turns into gestures.

On colorful Post-it notes, write down the first sentence of each paragraph.

Memorize the beginning and ending of your story. You need to know the first few lines so that you can launch into your story confidently when nervousness strikes. You also need to know the ending cold so that you can direct your pitch to that point and leave your audience satisfied.

Memorize any long expressions or essential language.

Rehearse in a closed room, without interruption. Rehearse standing up so that you can move freely. You are on your feet because your body as well as your mind has to learn the story.

SUMMARY

- Flesh out your stories with breakthrough moments that shaped you and your company.

- Assemble your pitch in three acts: set the stage (tell me), demo (show me), and transformation (sign me up).

- Authenticity + Humility = Likability. Be yourself.

- Put yourself in your audience's shoes. Why should people care?

- Master your live demo.

- End with an ask. You have wowed them. Now don't forget the reason you are there, be it funding, a new job, or a cause.

- Your pitch is a human connection, not a PowerPoint deck or a number of megabytes. Nurture and build it.

3

THE
ONE-MINUTE
PITCH

THE PITCH IS A SNAPSHOT OF THE BIGGER STORY

When I start a pitch session with a client, we never start working on the one-minute pitch right away. It is a bite-sized piece of a much larger pitch. Your pitch needs to encapsulate the bigger story of your idea, product, or business. It needs to be packaged in the most digestible way for audiences with short attention spans that are easily distracted.

The effectiveness of your pitch will reverberate. If it's memorable, which is what we are striving for, it will be retained and repeated by your audience, whether this is a potential investor or a large group of customers.

Your pitch is your brand. You must be able to communicate it in seconds, in shorter formats, and across multimedia platforms. The media have imposed formats: a 3-minute piece, a 60-minute feature, a 10-second sound bite. "Companies must learn how to publish, listen, and converse in a very fragmented media world," says Tom Forenski, former journalist and Silicon Valley blogger.[1] Being able to communicate quickly and effectively will ensure that you get your most important points across no matter what the length of the conversation.

I learned how to craft the perfect pitch through trial and error. When I worked for the French radio station France Info, we had to tell our stories in 40 seconds. The outcome of a cricket match between India and Pakistan? Forty seconds. A bomb blast that killed a family? Forty seconds. A profile of an entrepreneur? Forty seconds. The story had to be boiled down to its key elements even if everything seemed important. What helped? Our editors' mantra: "One idea, one sentence; one sentence, one idea."

When you work with such a minute-driven format, you learn that there is just so much you can do and say in a few seconds. So you need to make a choice. You can't tell everything, so what do you focus on?

Here are a few questions to get you thinking:

- Selling a product: How does your product solve a need?

- Selling a business: How does your business fit into the market?

- Selling yourself: What do you offer?

EXERCISE

How to Go for the Right Sound Bite

But how does one make that decision? Take a moment to think about the most memorable ways to describe what you are trying to get across. Think in terms of what makes your business or product newsworthy. Is it the fastest? Does it save the most money? Is it the most dependable? Is it great fun to use? Is it convenient?

What are you known for? Why do your users, clients, or customers love you?

Come up with three attributes.

When business executives ask me how in the world they can summarize what they do so quickly, I tell them about the countless entrepreneurs and CEOs who fail right out of the gate because they don't hook me right away. But take heart: a one-minute pitch doesn't happen overnight. It can take hours, days, or even months to craft a pitch that conveys the spark that motivates them and fuels their business, a pitch that shows how a real-world problem can be solved, how the company plans to do that, and why we should care. It's much more difficult than crafting a one-hour presentation, where you have the luxury of time and space. So it's important for entrepreneurs to think thoroughly about their pitches. The more you've thought about it, the more you believe in it, and the more conviction you'll convey.

Here's an example:

Every day, 10 people die from unintentional drowning. We have developed a patent-pending bracelet that inflates when there is too much agitation in the water. Our solution reduces a child's risk of drowning by 90 percent compared to a lifesaving jacket.

EXERCISE
Your Turn: Look Through the Looking Glass

In one minute, tell a family member, friend, colleague, or whoever is handy about an important project at work, your volunteer efforts, a hobby, or a passion. Explain what you do, why it's important to you, why you find it interesting, and why they should, too. As legendary editor and writer Michael Korda says, "If it's something that your mother would understand, you're on the right track." This doesn't mean that you have to water it down or oversimplify it, but it does mean that you want to speak from a place of authenticity and true belief in what you are saying. This is key to a good pitch.

If your pitch is directed at a younger person, tailor it to that person and use dynamic, relatable language. In other words, everyone you test your short pitch on should be able to understand what you do and why it matters, and describe it to others.

It's good practice to pitch people you know well because they won't have a filter. They will tell you exactly what worked and what didn't, and why. Plus, if your pitch goes well, your mother or your father will be able to explain what you do at the next family dinner, and you'll be the star of the evening.

This is an exercise that I highly recommend. It helps you perfect a tight, colorful, and powerful presentation in an environment that is a lot less stressful than a pitch slam or boardroom, so that when you get to the real thing, you will have confidence both from feedback and from practicing your pitch multiple times.

BEAT THE CLOCK

For a one-minute pitch, time is your biggest enemy. How do you turn it to your advantage?

Managing your time will transform your pitch. To make the most of your one minute, stay silent for the first 3 seconds. Silence will focus the audience's attention on you. It is also a sign of confidence. Spend the next 10 seconds on your punchiest content and think about wrapping up at the 50-second mark. That will leave you enough time to stay composed.

Your one-minute pitch must be prepared, practiced, and polished to get people excited about what you do. Don't forget that your pitch to investors will be shared with their partners, so make it easy for them to repeat it.

A successful pitch will make people sit up and take notice. In those first few seconds, you want them to look up from their smartphones, stop checking their e-mail and Twitter accounts, and focus on you.

Preparing to make the perfect pitch is a three-step process:

- *Practice*. Practice sets you free. When you have your pitch down cold, your mind isn't burdened by what you have to say or how you have to say it. Practice sets you free to respond spontaneously while you're pitching. It enables you to convey your passion with greater authenticity.

- *Revise.* Revise your pitch based on feedback. The more feedback you get, the better your pitch will become. Welcome criticism. Invite it in. Only by doing so will you make your pitch as bulletproof as it can be.

- *Ask.* Be memorable. Your idea may be yours alone, but you will be sharing the stage and the attention that goes with it with others like you. Be the one the audience remembers.

And yes, a minute is more than enough time to convey the crucial details about what you do—and what you are asking for.

When I ask clients to take an ambitious idea and encapsulate it in a few sentences, they look at me like I'm crazy. They think that a minute can't possibly contain the complexity of their offer—whether they are selling themselves, a product, or a service—and they complain that it's simply not possible to cram everything they need to say into such a short period of time.

However, they are missing the point. An elevator pitch isn't about squeezing their whole business concept into a short form and trying to speed-deliver it. Instead, it's about finding the one thing that makes your idea really incredible and opens the door to a longer conversation between you and your target audience.

Broken down into its essence, a pitch is just a story. Let's look at the main components of a story: the hook, the structure, the essence, and the ending.

EXERCISE
Organize Your Pitch

Purpose: A one-minute pitch should be simple and easy to understand and should generate more questions. Calibrate your pitch, organize it, and rehearse it.

First step: Pick 1, 2, 3, or 4.

1. Think about your latest car purchase. Make a case for why you bought that particular car.

2. Think about your favorite magazine subscription. What makes it worthwhile?

3. Are you more of a Facebook, Instagram, Twitter, or Pinterest person? How do you use it, and why do you like it?

4. What was your last holiday destination? Why would you recommend it?

Pitch your car, your magazine, your social media platform, or your holiday destination in one minute. Write down your pitch and say it out loud to get a feel for the flow.

Second step:
A one-minute pitch should be very organized. Check the corresponding boxes if you said:

- ❑ Who you are

- ❑ The name of the car, magazine, platform, or place

- ❑ The relevant character

- ❑ What motivated your choice

- ❑ Why it's exciting

- ❑ Why your audience should consider it and perhaps adopt it

Third step:
Practice makes perfect. Rewrite your pitch, following the checked box guidelines. Read it out loud again. How does it sound now?

FROM AN IDEA TO A PITCH

Here are three ideas to remember when pitching.

In the first 5 to 10 seconds, tell us who you are and what you do. Now that you have my attention, use the next 15 to 20 seconds to capture my interest by framing the problem. Keep me hooked by providing the solution in no more than 20 seconds. Keep me there by adding pressing or urgent information. In the last 10 seconds, ask me what I can do for you.

Here are three frameworks you can use for your one-minute pitch.

Pitch Perfect: Fill In the Blanks

Here is a good general template you can use. Fill in the blanks with your story, which will become your pitch.

Hello, my name is . . . *[First and last name, followed by short title. Nothing else.]*

I am an x *[engineer, marketer, designer, investor]* creating the next generation of x platform connecting x and x that does x. *[Keep it short and simple: two sentences maximum.]*

Have you tried to do x and x recently? *[Let them speak. A question is great to generate interest and to*

show that you care about them—and are not just fo-
cused on spitting out your pitch, regardless of who is
in front of you.]

We have observed that the *x* market prevents *x*
and *x* from doing *x*. It limits *x* from getting *xyz*. *[Define*
the problem.]

Here is what we propose to solve that problem.
[It should be very simple and logical. Just offer one
solution. Don't dive into too many details.]

We developed *x* tool that *x* and *x* can use to *xyz*.
[Be specific if it's an app, software, a physical prod-
uct, or a service. Too many times, entrepreneurs for-
get to say what it is.]

The timing is great because the market is *x [mar-*
ket size] or we have had *x* growth *[traction showing*
that your business is taking off incredibly fast] or we
have *xxx* backing us *[social proof to show that credi-*
ble advisors or other investors are backing you].

Our team has credibility because *[show that you*
have done it successfully in the past or have a domain
expertise that is uniquely relevant to your market].

Do you have among your contacts someone who
has faced *xyz* or who could introduce us to *x* or set
up a meeting with *x*? *[Finish with a clear ask: buy-in,*
a recommendation, or an introduction. Don't finish
your pitch without closure.]

Here are suggestions concerning your delivery:

Hello, my name is . . . *[Speak loudly and clearly.]*

I am an *x* creating the next generation of *x* platform connecting *x* and *x*. *[Pause and breathe, because, as the listener, I need some time to absorb what you have just told me.]*

Have you tried to do *x* and *x* recently? *[Pause.]*

We have observed that the *x* market prevents *x* and *x* from doing *x*. It limits *x* from getting *xyz*. *[Become animated. Show that it's a real problem.]*

Here is what we propose to solve that problem. We developed *x* tool that *x* and *x* can use to *xyz*. *[Speak passionately.]*

The timing is great because the market is *x or* we have had *x* growth *[slow down when sharing numbers] or* we have *xxx* backing us. *[Articulate clearly.]*

Our team has credibility because . . . *[Speak confidently.]*

Do you have among your contacts someone who has faced *xyz* or who could introduce us to *x* or set up a meeting with *x*? *[Finish strong. Look them in the eye.]*

A pitch is about giving people a glimpse of what their tomorrow will look like, thanks to you. It involves telling a story about what it is you are doing, why you are doing it, and how you intend to finish it. So, much like a reporter composing a lead, focus on the what, why, and how.

EXERCISE
Know What You Are About to Do

Do a self-check. Can you ensure that you have a one-sentence answer to the following six questions?

- What are you presenting? (an idea, a new product, a prototype, an update, a team, etc.)

- Why are you presenting? (what your purpose is, what you want to achieve)

- Who is your audience? (investors, customers, team members)

- Where are you presenting? (a meeting room, a conference room, a boardroom, a theater)

- How long are you presenting? (10 seconds, 1 minute, 3 minutes, 5 minutes, 10 minutes, 30 minutes, 60 minutes)

- How are you presenting? (standing, sitting, bicycling—Google has a seven-seat conference bike)

Perfect Pitches

Here are a couple of examples:

Hi, my name is Sharma, I am an ex-Nexus Google engineer. I have been ordering chicken kungpao from all the Chinese restaurants because I didn't know how to read the menu in Mandarin. I intend to create an application that translates the menu from Mandarin to English in real time by scanning the menu and showing me that I can get zucchini with pepper sauce and tofu with pineapple and cashews. Jamie Oliver just invested two million dollars of his own money in our app. I am raising another two million dollars for the development of this app to help others expand their culinary horizons.

Hi, I am Jing, a former child specialist working at Berkeley. I have invented an app for children to learn how to tell time. Children have had no concrete way of learning how to tell what time it is in other parts of the world. I developed an application that allows children to understand how the compass works as a way of telling whether it's night or day in Shanghai, Rio, or Johannesburg. We all know that it's crucial to track time, but for kids, knowing that there is a huge world out there to explore is what's key. We have been number one in the Apple Store in more than 50 countries, and we were voted Parent's Best. Please help me fund an app that helps kids all over the world.

The Power of the One-Sentence Pitch

If you had to describe your company in a single sentence, what would it be?

Summarize in one sentence what you do. The shorter, the better. You have to make it simple if people are to be able to repeat it to their partners, colleagues, bosses, or friends. This sentence should appear at the top of your business plan or on the first slide of your PowerPoint presentation. (There is a Facebook One-Sentence Startup Pitches group with more than 7,000 members, who post hilarious one-sentences pitches.)

The following examples illustrate how to convey very distinct points succinctly. These pitches capture only the bare essentials.

Examples:

What Is It?

- Our fitness app is an online platform that pairs personal trainers with gym goers who want to lose weight.

- Our startup provides machine learning software that controls the electrical switches for your home depending on your preferences.

- Our startup is a social platform that lets users edit, upload, and share pictures of all types.

- We build in-store touchscreen kiosks for consumers and stylists to find new collections and share fashion and hair inspiration.

- Our startup is a service that helps users track and discover local chefs.

For Whom?

- Our product is a child-safe digital advertising platform.

- We are a loyalty card program for restaurants and retailers.

- Our startup connects brands with video production professionals.

- Our solution enables prospective buyers and renters to search local brokers directly.

For What?

- Our startup is a home for on-demand radio shows, DJ mixes, and podcasts.

- It's a cloud-based platform that helps advertisers and marketers create videos.

- We are the largest broker and online auctioneer for secondhand cars in Canada.

Analogies can work, but don't abuse them. They have to be very simple in order to work:

- "Pandora for niche music genres and indie bands."

- "Squarespace with open-source software and templates."

A well-thought-out pitch can help you get in the door. You have only one shot at making a good impression. Make it count.

Now let's zoom in on the essential indicators that show that you are not creating an imaginary world for yourself.

EXERCISE

Show Traction

Check the proof of traction that applies to you and conveys exciting momentum:

❑ Creating your company

Example: "We have finished our website, registered as an LLC, and received our first business credit card."

❑ Website traffic

Example: Don't say: "We have 100,000 users."

Do say: "We signed up 100,000 users in only 45 days."

❑ Paying customers

Example: "We sign up 1,000 paying users every day."

❑ User growth

Example: "In the past three weeks, we have added 10,000 new users to our site and are doubling that rate every day."

❏ Sales

Examples: "We have been generating *x* revenue since our product's introduction in South Korea six months ago, and it will launch in the United States in three months."

"We increased sales by 50 percent over two years."

❏ Partners

Examples: "We have just received $50 million in venture funding."

"We have raised more than $40 million in a third round of funding led by Facebook investors."

❏ New companies coming on board

Example: "Our product is available in 680 retail stores."

❏ Key hires

Example: "We have hired the former CTO of Google."

❏ New hires

Example: "We grew from 12 people to 200 in a year."

(continued)

❑ Published work

Example: "I authored a blog post that was viewed more than 5,000 times in two days."

What other examples of traction do you have that are not on this list?

Teamwork

Investors tell me that what they care most about is the team.

Focus on the aspects of your and your team's background that are most salient to the promised success of your company. It's great that you have a degree from Harvard, but if you are in the Internet of Things for animal wearables, that may not be the most relevant piece of information people want to hear from you. But if you are in the Voice over Internet Protocol (online video calls) business, referring to your telecom engineering degree gives you credibility. By showing proof of your expertise in the domain you are addressing, you are convincing your subject that you know what you are talking about.

It's always best to combine your title with a well-known brand.

Example:

For a marketing platform: "Our team includes the former VP of marketing at Verizon and the head of digital branding at Ogilvy."

Social Proof

We live in a world in which knowing "how many contacts we have in common on LinkedIn" or checking our friends' friends' profiles on Facebook creates the tangible connection we need in order to feel that someone is trustworthy. So telling someone that you worked at Yahoo! together, went to the same college, or married her cousin puts you on her friend map.

You are legitimized by having been endorsed by someone who is known to your subject.

Which is your social proof?

❏ You went to school together.

❏ You come from the same hometown.

❏ You have the same team of advisors.

❏ A celebrity is using your product.

❏ The *New York Times* has been covering your story from the beginning.

❏ You have raised $50 million on Kickstarter.

❏ You worked on Hillary Clinton's team.

❏ You have among your investors one who has invested in startups with the largest current valuations.

Your social proof should boost your credibility in a context in which everyone is ready to say whatever he can to capture attention.

Assuming that you have explained yourself, established credibility, and generated interest, finish your pitch with an ask.

The Ask

- *How much are you raising?* "I am raising *x* amount of money." Say it simply and directly. Investors have different windows of investments. You may be in some people's sweet spot, but not in others'.

- *What is your funding round?* "I am raising seed money (under $500,000), Series A (under $5 million), Series B ($10 to 15 million), or Series C (it varies from company to company)."

- *Are you in a hurry?* "I would like to discuss this further this week or the following week, if you are available." "I am raising x by the end of the year." Or "I am preparing for next year." Mentioning your timeline puts a reference on the table.

Should you share everything in a pitch? What shouldn't you say?

Sharing stories that are too personal—about your private life—or venting about your former boss or other investors is not wise. For a first meeting with a potential investor, any confidential information, including patent details or revenue numbers, can be left out of the presentation deck. You can keep those sheets for the end of the presentation if the meeting takes longer than expected or for the next meeting, should you pursue the conversation. That's also why doing your homework on investors with ethical standards and good reputations is crucial in your pitch work.

When is it appropriate to bring up an NDA (non-disclosure agreement)? Some people who come from the corporate world are used to signing NDAs. You can't ask an investor to sign an NDA on your very first pitch, however. In early-stage conversations, it may deter interest in your company. Sure, as an entrepreneur, you don't want someone stealing your idea. However, "If you go to VC firms with a brilliant idea but tell them to sign a non-disclosure agreement, most will tell you to get lost. That shows how much a mere idea is worth. The market price is less than the inconvenience of signing an NDA," says Paul Graham, founder of Y Combinator.[2]

How much should you tell them? "Some of them may one day be funding your competitors," says Graham. "I think the best plan is not to be overly secretive, but not to tell them everything, either. After all, as most VCs say, they're more interested in the people than the ideas. The main reason they want to talk about your idea is to judge you, not the idea. So as long as you seem like you know what you're doing, you can probably keep a few things back from them."

You shouldn't worry about someone stealing or copying your idea from a short pitch, as executing and implementing your idea cannot be copied in five minutes. Trust yourself with your idea.

A good time to require an NDA is when investors want to invest in your company and will be privy, for example, to the algorithms related to your trade. Speak in general terms during the exploratory phase. Before you explain your revenue projections in detail, display your operational expenses, or share your cash flow, ask for an NDA. But it is possible to raise capital without all those documents in place.

FROM A GOOD PITCH TO A PERFECT PITCH

Now that you have your one-minute pitch down, how can you turn it into a perfect one? Moreover, how do you customize it for different audiences?

Many entrepreneurs forget that a pitch that works for one person doesn't necessarily work for another. A pitch is not a fixed text. "What's your story?" is another way of asking, "Who are you?" What works for one investor may not work for another. What works onstage may not work in a boardroom. What works in Berlin won't work in Salt Lake City.

Your pitch should be customized to the person you are pitching. That means having a keen understanding of the person and what she wants and being able to convey that within the first few sentences.

The better your pitch fits into your listener's perspective, the greater your odds. But always tell the truth. Your story is rich enough without your having to embroider it. You have to be aware of your audience's perspective, its context, and who its members are. Pitching to someone who shares the same perspective can be really powerful.

Example: "Do you remember the last time you went to a music concert and were irritated because at the time of checkout, you had to pay a $12 fee on a $40 ticket?

127

No one likes paying extra fees on their concert tickets. Our app saves you 60 percent on fees."

I recommend having three to five one-minute pitches that are well prepared, practiced, and polished. The more versatile you are, the more confident and adaptable you will be in your delivery. Knowing what to say in any circumstances will allow for more focus.

Having different pitches also comes in handy at parties, when you need to quickly explain what you do for a second time in front of someone you've already told and the new person in the circle.

Here are other ways of sharing perspective:

- *Say a few words in the local language,* whether it's tech speak or a regional saying. Remember Mark Zuckerberg stunning China by speaking Mandarin at Tsinghua University, China's MIT.

- *Start with a question.* "Have you ever . . . ?" "Have you noticed . . . ?" and "How do you . . . ?" work well. All the better if the question is related to current events or hot news topics. To do it well, wait for people to start answering or even mumbling. Otherwise, it looks too prepared.

- *Show a picture or video or listen to music.* Edward Tufte, the data visualization statistician, starts his workshops by playing a musical piece in a dark room.

Context matters.

EXERCISE
Assess Your Pitch Progress

On a scale of 1–10, how was your:

- Pace?

- Breathing?

- Pausing?

- Clarity?

- Memorization?

Watch and assess other pitches online. The more you see, the more you'll be able to give yourself critical feedback.

PITCH FOR SUCCESS: PUTTING IT ALL TOGETHER

A few years ago, I trained an entrepreneur who did a demo at the Web Summit tech conference in Dublin, attended by 20,000 investors and entrepreneurs. We worked on practicing and rehearsing his pitch dozens of times so that he would be ready. Little did we know that the right time for his pitch would be at a crowded bar late at night, but it was. He landed six new clients for his software business. Born in India, my client did something that he had initially found daunting: successfully pitched European clients for his U.S.-based business. And he did it even while speaking over loud music. He was concise and to the point, knowing that as the evening wore on, people would become increasingly inebriated and have less bandwidth to focus on business conversation. But he did it.

How? He practiced; revised based on the feedback he received from me and others; focused on who he was, what he had to offer, and how it would solve a problem; and left with an ask.

You can, too.

Remember, your pitch should sound conversational, like you are talking to a friend or colleague about something that truly excites you. You're bringing your listeners along on a ride. It's not a master class or an educational course. It's meant to generate excitement.

EXERCISE

Find the Perfect Place to Practice

Practice anywhere that works for you, but you should be alone so that you can concentrate. Ideally, you should be able to move around comfortably. Devote some time to finding the perfect spot.

EXERCISE

Find the Perfect Time to Practice

Pitching in two weeks? Schedule 10 minutes a day on your calendar. If it's on your calendar, you're more likely to do it. Right before lunch is a good time because you have the lunch deadline. To maximize your concentration, turn off your phone notifications.

SUMMARY

What to remember when working on your perfect one-minute pitch:

- It is a short story about you and what you do.
- It should be customized for your audience.

- Make your first 10 seconds count. Establish your expertise. What do you bring to the table?

- It is about providing a solution to a problem that plagues those in your audience. Put it in terms that they can relate to. Make them care.

- Keep it simple and to the point. Eliminate jargon.

- End with an ask. What do you want from those in your audience? What do you want to leave them with?

- Practice, practice, practice.

- Revise based on feedback.

4

KNOW YOUR AUDIENCE

S pending hours practicing your elevator pitch is key to connecting with a potential investor, winning the opportunity to present a more detailed business plan, and receiving the holy grail: funding. If you don't succeed, you have to keep pitching. This often means going back to the drawing board. What parts of your pitch worked? What parts could be improved?

Your audience, which is often made up of venture capitalists, also finds the pitching process frustrating because only a tiny fraction of pitches lead to the financial due diligence analysis of a company. And even fewer lead to a deal that will have a chance of scaling to a multibillion-dollar valuation. Great deals are hard to come by.

"The number of pitches we see has quadrupled from what we used to see 10 years ago," says Jeff Clavier, founder and managing partner of SoftTech VC, a seed firm in Silicon Valley. "In '04, you barely had 50 or 100 entrepreneurs trying to raise money for consumer start-ups or B2B startups. We get anywhere from 2,500 to

3,000 pitches by e-mail, and we'll meet about 20 percent of the companies, so roughly between 400 and 600 meetings . . . it might be a thousand. We only invest in four or five companies per quarter or 15 to 20 companies per year."[1]

To increase their odds of receiving funding, entrepreneurs must realize that the pitch is absolutely crucial, even if it means weeks—or months—of diligent preparation.

Investors also find themselves pitching. After meetings with entrepreneurs, they pitch new ideas to their fund partners. They pitch new stories to their limited partners to get more funding. When the fund is coming to an end, they have to raise a new round of money and pitch their current investments again. And among angel investors, angel groups, mutual funds, hedge funds, venture capital firms, and corporate venture investors, there is a great deal of competition for deals. It's not just capital venture investors. Investors also have to pitch to encourage entrepreneurs to work with them and accept their investment.

One of my clients is an investment firm, a small fund that has been active in the Valley for many years. It wanted more inbound pitches and higher referrals. I asked the firm's leaders to tell stories about how they guide their portfolio companies.

Here are some examples:

"We have a weekly meeting with our companies, provide them with enough introductions to get them to the front of the line, and are always available on our cell phones, should they need advice or guidance."

"We tell our companies about the bad days—and there will be bad days—and how we will help them through."

New funds, old funds, well-established funds—the pitch wheel is always spinning. Your pitch must accommodate constant changes in the business landscape.

Every day there is new information on your competition and on the investors you are trying to reach, all of it available immediately. As an entrepreneur, you must have a better sense of your market, better hires with new capabilities, and a better take on the ideas that bubble to the surface.

THE UNSPOKEN RULES: THE LAY OF THE LAND

There is no rulebook for making it in Silicon Valley.

But deciphering the unspoken rules takes some time, and it is even harder to do if you are from another country. There are rules for pitching in the Valley, where the investors are kings and queens. They offer their verdicts in the form of checks for the luckiest entrepreneurs. For the others, it's back to the drawing board.

Silicon Valley is a scary court where entrepreneurs are subject to the harsh judgment of investors, advisors, business angels, and their competitors. There is no one to represent or defend them, which makes pitching to investors even more frustrating when you are ignorant of the unspoken rules. I have worked with clients who "lost" three months after arriving in Silicon Valley. They couldn't get a single meeting with investors.

Arriving in Silicon Valley with no network and no introduction to powerful investors is incredibly difficult. Benchmark Capital, for example, a Dropbox, eBay, Instagram, Yelp, and Zillow investor, has a spartan website with only one hyperlink, which directs visitors to the Twitter feed of its portfolio companies.

One of the companies I mentored at 500 Startups printed custom books with the face of the investor it wanted to reach out to on the cover. Company representatives would wait for him in the lobby of his hotel and hand him the book. The investor was more than a little surprised but agreed to a meeting.

There are less dramatic ways to meet investors in Silicon Valley. However, to build your network and get new introductions, you need to focus your search. Look for three to five investors and track them down.

Here's how:

- Connect with a startup incubator or accelerator, private or government-funded. It will separate you from the pack, and you will score introductions through that network. Participate in its demo days.

- Attend speaker events, startup conferences, and book signings. Spot your favorite investor having lunch or breakfast at a café? Pitch him for a few seconds. Get his e-mail address, do a follow-up, and ask for further introductions.

- Research companies that have received funding from investors you are looking to connect with. Contact them and ask for introductions. Check their social media pages. Browse LinkedIn. Many partners at venture capital firms blog, too. Once you have the contact, nurture it. But be respectful of everyone's time.

- Follow the "great minds think alike" rule. Find investors whose vision aligns with yours. They will be more receptive to your pitch.

"Preaching to the choir" has never been so current.

- Ask your local network what people in town you should meet. That network could be your alumni association, your foreign-country chamber of commerce, your kid's school, your sports association, or your former company. Ask for introductions. Always get people's e-mail addresses and business cards. Don't wait for them to contact you. I like the e-card app NoBizCard. You just enter someone's e-mail address and send your e-card with your contact information.

- Attend classes at Stanford Continuing Studies or at entrepreneurship centers. Connect with fellow students before and after class.

- Sign up for relevant mailing lists to receive notifications of upcoming events.

Working on developing your network is key to investor funding.

"I need someone to be vetted by someone I respect," says Sean Jacobsohn of Norwest Venture Partners, a

EXERCISE

Your Circles of Influence

Take a pen and paper. Draw the circles in which you are the most socially active, whether professional, academic, or personal. Some people from your school circle will overlap with your work circle.

At each intersection where circles overlap, write the names of the last three successful introductions that were enabled by those circles.

What else can you do to make the most of your network?

EXERCISE

Use the Tech Press for Research

Find the latest *Inc.* magazine list of the 5,000 fastest-growing companies that recently received funding or the *San Jose Mercury News* venture capital survey.

Short-list 20 to 100 companies in your field.

Visit their websites and find out who their investors are. Read their blogs and social media pages.

Check their investors' profiles on LinkedIn.

You should end up with a list of at least three to five investors to reach out to.

EXERCISE
Target the Best Audience

Do your homework and pitch only investors that you know could potentially invest in you.

- Is the potential market opportunity large enough for their investment model?

- Is your market one of their prime targets?

- Is their typical investment size what you are looking for?

- Is their location what you are looking for?

  Ask them:

- What have you learned from working with entrepreneurs?

- Have you had to fire anyone? How did you feel about it?

- I have noticed that you invested in a couple of companies in the *xyz* space. What kind of investments are you interested in?

venture capital firm in Silicon Valley. "If they can't get to me through a connection that I respect, it's a sign to me that they're not very resourceful people, and maybe I shouldn't meet them. As a startup, you need to be able to get in front of people through other people. It's not just fund-raising, but it's for customers and partners. If you can't leverage your resources and connections to get in front of people, you will have difficulty building a great business. So it's a signal for me. I can't respond to every inbound. I have to be very selective. My focus is on the companies I call, not the ones that call me. Seventy-five percent of my time is focused on companies that I am reaching out to. Twenty-five percent of the time I will leave open for vetted inbounds from people I respect, which doesn't leave me a lot of time to meet the random company, but I will make the time."[2]

The Right Target

Most investors say that most of their deals come from re-ferrals or repeat entrepreneurs. If you're new to Silicon Valley or you're a first-time entrepreneur, this may seem daunting. Do your research.

"Once you know whom you're targeting, figure out how to reach out to them through a common connec-tion," says Jeff Clavier, founder and managing partner of

SoftTech VC, "someone who knows you and knows the investor who will vouch for you. What you're seeking is an accredited transfer."[3]

Once you have done your research—read company or investor profiles, interviews of your targets, and all the online literature you can find—and identified the best potential investors in your field, it's time to write your e-mail query. The perfect e-mail pitch is short enough to pique the investor's interest by tapping into the personal connection you have in common and the key areas she is interested in. Like you, investors get tons of e-mail and ignore or erase unopened ones at the end of the week. Why should they open yours?

How to Pitch Investors by E-mail

The same techniques that work for investors also apply to any professional looking to get attention by e-mail, whether an entrepreneur, a sales professional, or a job seeker.

Your Subject Line

A good subject line may not get you an appointment, but a bad subject line will definitely prevent you from getting one. The subject line is your opportunity to trigger a reaction in the sender: open this e-mail.

Remember, it's all about the personal connection.

- "Friend of/ Intro from xxx at Google"; "Met at the TechCrunch party/ Booth no. 45"; "4th of July party at Sequoia Capital"; "Lean In discussion in Palo Alto"

    By focusing on a human person and a personal relationship, you will be more likely to get attention than with an anonymous company name alone. If you've spoken with the person, it's good to remind him of where you met. If you haven't met him, the name of the event will suffice.

- "*Your startup name* from Bordeaux in San Francisco this week"

    Referring to your place of origin may work, especially if the investor invests in that region. Mentioning your timing is also helpful.

If you don't have a personal connection, you need to include the most salient detail of your business that may capture attention.

- "*Your startup name*: founded by ex-Uber CTO"

    The investor may not know your startup, but she definitely knows the other company and would like to know what you are up to.

Dropping a famous name may help place yours on her map.

- "*Your startup name*: Delivering automated presentations in seconds"

  Mention your name and the problem you are solving.

- "Traction: how we grew from 700 to 3,000 users in one week"

  Refer to the promise of your startup.

Once you have met with an investor or any other important person, send a follow-up e-mail with an attention-getting subject line:

- "Let's connect and have lunch Thursday, June 25, or Friday, July 5, at Madera Café on Sand Hill Road"

  Propose coffee, lunch, or drinks. Meeting in person makes it much easier to form a bond. But try to keep it short and sweet. Suggest a 10- to 30-minute meeting. Everyone has limited time.

- "*Your startup name*: Catch-up"

- A question: "When will you be back from Singapore?"

EXERCISE

Mine Past Introductions

Select the last three e-mail introductions a friend or a connection made for you.

- How did they start their intro?

- What words did they use to describe what you do?

- How did they speak about your expertise?

- What did they ask the person they introduced you to to do?

Reading how others introduce you or talk about you is a great way to help yourself see what's most important to others.

Use that information in your next batch of e-mails.

Develop a Punchy E-mail Pitch

An introductory e-mail should catch people's attention. Make sure you send the right e-mail to the right person and don't blow your opportunity with a careless mistake.

- Use the person's first name or nickname.

Silicon Valley is not formal. First names are expected. Jeff Clavier says, "If someone calls me Jean-François, it means that he doesn't know me."[4] He would be less likely to respond.

- Mention the friend or acquaintance you have in common.

    Check LinkedIn, Facebook, or any groups you have on social networks. Look for any connection you two might share and for every opportunity to show social proof.

- Cite the person's background, an investment, or an interest he has that shows that you took the time to learn about him. "I have seen that you . . ."

Determine what other companies the person has invested in, why, how much, and during how many rounds to avoid any conflict of interest if the person were to invest in you. Because you are also looking for her expertise, check her operational experience running a business and whether she took her company public.

Here's an example:

Hi Aaron,

We are both friends with *x* from *x [show personal connection]*. I have been working on developing a product called *x* that does *x [cut to the chase about what your product or business is]* and saw that you *x [cite relevant background].*

Our product lets you *[solution to a problem].* We have over *x* users, and we have grown by *x [market size or traction].* We previously raised $*x* from *x [cite investors for social proof].*

Before *x [name of the company],* I started *x [previous company],* which was acquired by *x [buyer].*

I would love to meet and show you *x. [Insert the link to your website or a free trial or attach supporting material. Make sure that the link works and that no password is required.]*

Best regards,

Karen

(e-mail address)

(cell phone number)

MAKE YOUR BUSINESS WRITING PERSONAL

Your pitch should be written to be memorized. Whether it's an e-mail, a presentation deck, an executive summary, or a business plan, the writing style should be simple and concise, without jargon.

Here are a few rules:

1. *Make them feel good.* Don't behave as though you are the smartest person in the room. Create a positive emotional experience. You need to get your investor to think, "This is a person I'd like to work with. This is a product I'd like to try. This is a company that is going to make a lot of money."

   I advised one of my French clients not to start his pitch with "Let me explain this to you," which can sound patronizing. Use the appropriate tone of voice. Be confident and assertive, but do not sound like "I know it all."

2. *Surprise them.* If your product is really beautiful and easy to use, then show it off to investors and wait for them to say, "Oh, that's really cool." Go for the unexpected.

3. *Transport them.* Show them your vision of a better future. Use "Imagine" or "What if?" What intriguing question are you trying to address?

4. *Solve their problems in a timely manner.* Send just before dinnertime: "We have discovered the easiest way in the world to eat healthily."

Send just before a long holiday weekend: "Have you ever had problems loading books on your e-readers? Is the price right? When traveling overseas, can you find what you want? What if you could buy all the books you wanted from any store in the world without having to enter your credit card information multiple times?"

5. *Use plain English*. Keep it simple. There's no need for flowery language or adventurous formulas.

Here are some examples:

"Printing photos from mobile phones is a difficult and complex process."

"There are no halal stores in Japan."

"Going to the store to buy a calling card for Mexico is time-consuming and expensive."

Avoid hyperbole. Do not say:

"We have been working on a revolutionary product."

"Our new groundbreaking technology is changing lives."

"We are constantly pushing the envelope to build breakthrough machines."

"We are manufacturing state-of-the art medical systems."

"Our best-in-class practices will contribute to the advancement of growth in key areas of importance."

"Our cutting-edge technologies will change the world."

6. *Get to the point.* Don't beat around the bush. Lengthy explanations won't help people understand you any better. Don't focus on the underlying technology.

7. *Grammar matters.* Use spell check but don't depend on it. Make sure your grammar is correct. Have someone else proofread your message if necessary. People are very quick to notice mistakes and may dismiss a message if they spot too many errors or repetitions.

8. *Focus.* One idea, one sentence. One sentence, one idea. Move logically from one to the next.

9. *Avoid buzzwords or jargon.* If your field requires a specialized word or two, use it, but make sure you're explaining it for a layperson. Audiences

tune out jargon that doesn't mean anything to them. Find a synonym that's closest to what it truly means. Be accessible.

10. *State what you do in positive terms.* Show yourself in the best light. But always tell the truth. Don't be arrogant, but don't be too humble, either. You want to be confident in your achievements and abilities, but with concrete evidence to back it up. Do not frame things negatively. Don't say, "We don't have this capability."

EXERCISE
Run Assessments

Which one of the following assessments is the closest to what your idea or product is?

- A tiny tweak to something that's already in existence

- A new feature or enhancement to an existing product/service/company/business

- A major new area of an existing product/service/company/business

(continued)

- An entirely new but small and simple project

- An entirely new but large and possibly complex project

- An organizational, directional, or philosophical change to an existing organization

- A new organization

EXERCISE
Create Your LinkedIn Profile

As an entrepreneur, you need to have an updated LinkedIn profile. Investors and recruiters will research you online. Besides the professional photo and catchy headline, how do you create a stellar summary of yourself?

In the opening paragraph, describe the work that you do. Include your years of experience and your expertise in solving specific problems.

In the second paragraph, select a few impressive accomplishments and give a brief overview of your previous experience that led you to where you are now.

In the final paragraph, describe your working style to set yourself apart from others. Add any out-of-the box qualifications that are work-related. Conclude by explaining what you are looking for: a meeting, new opportunities, business contacts, or something else.

- Does it grab attention from the opening sentence?

- Did you break it up to make it visually easy to read?

- Did you use the 2,000 characters allotted?

- Did you use the first person? It's a far more personal approach than using the third.

EXERCISE
Create the About Page

The About page is the number one page viewed on a website after the home page. It's an opportunity to tell your story. Like your pitch itself, it should communicate what you and your business are about: who you are, the problem you are solving for your clients,

(continued)

155

what makes you unique, your expertise, your location, and so on. It should be a few paragraphs, not an essay.

It's often good to start with your pitch and build out. Think of it as your personal mission statement.

Here are some ideas to get you started:

- In 2008, I left law school and started my business in retail.

- I appeared on a list of the Top 5 Most Influential Mobile Experts.

- I won a Pulitzer Prize for . . .

- With nearly 20 years of experience in . . .

- My name is *x*, and this is what I love:

- I am an engineer based in Atlanta, who believes most in . . .

EXERCISE
Create a Testimonial Page

Conveying trust is critical. Testimonials should be exact quotes, with the names and titles of the people

who provided them. For the most effective testimonials, ask your contributors to answer the following
questions:

- Why do you use our product?

- What problem does it solve for you?

- What do you like about the user experience? Why
  would you use it again?

- To whom would you recommend it and why?

THE UNSPOKEN RULES: FOR NON-NATIVE ENGLISH SPEAKERS

If you are from another country, there are many wild and
mysterious rules in Silicon Valley. The West Coast still
represents the frontier, a place where everything is possible, offering pioneers a new beginning that allows them
to create a new story for themselves. Navigating the
pitching process is an arduous exercise. Pitches are char-
acterized by a high degree of uncertainty, as investors
must evaluate the business opportunity and the entrepreneur's ability to execute based on limited information.
It doesn't matter where you are from. But pitching your

startup as a non-native English speaker demands even greater imagination and discipline.

Silicon Valley is a busy hive, with many engineers, entrepreneurs, and adventurous minds from all over the world, drawn by the same dreams that attract so many. Fifty percent of the startups created in Silicon Valley have at least one founder who was born overseas.

Sean Jacobsohn, an investor with Norwest Venture Partners, defines Silicon Valley as "a laboratory where experiments happen," which puts entrepreneurs and founders in the unique position of trying things that they could not attempt where they came from because of cultural and social pressure, administrative barriers, or the limited size of the market.[5]

A laptop and a Wi-Fi connection are all it takes to found a company, and the odds are in the entrepreneur's favor. According to David Blumberg, managing partner of Blumberg Capital, the cost of early-stage entrepreneurship has dropped significantly.[6] Investors say that it is easier and more capital-efficient to start an information technology company, get the product to market, and reach large and expanding markets than ever before.

Most of the non-native-English-speaking entrepreneurs I have worked with are brilliant engineers and mathematicians, used to dealing with numbers, data, and complex systems. When they find themselves onstage, trying to explain their business in a few minutes, they often use too many numbers, abstract language, and overloaded PowerPoint presentations. Explaining big data, how the cloud works, or the latest tricks for learning language coding requires a great deal of imagination and agility on the part of the presenter.

How do I advise my non-native-English-speaking clients to tell their stories? Animate your numbers with a character to illustrate your point; show us what a product did for you; tell us about the journey that led you to that conclusion. Don't come in with a 50-slide presentation. Don't open your pitch without pausing between long sentences. Don't tell us about your PhD or your field of research or apologize for being here. Quantify your product or your progress with metrics. Don't shy away from talking about money.

"We have a very sort of dollars-and-cents attitude, where the need is often expressed in terms of dollars," said Richard Zolezzi, a lawyer at Nixon Peabody. "People normally expect something that is couched in monetary terms as well. Or at least metrics. Sometimes people from other countries, culturally, aren't quite as comfortable speaking in those terms."[7]

Even if your product is technical, there is always a human way to explain it. Don't believe that your English is an obstacle. "We sometimes don't put non-native

English speakers on stage not because of their language issue but because they don't present well," an international economic forum founder told me.

I once had a client whose accent was very thick and who constantly mixed up the pronouns *she* and *he*. I had her focus on her strengths—her charismatic personality, her ability to speak loudly and clearly, and her effective body language—to convey her message. After some training sessions, she managed to explain the achievements in the company's last quarter. If you appeal to those in your audience with sincerity—and communicate what you yourself truly believe in—they will listen.

How do you break into Silicon Valley as a non-American?

Create Your Profile

- Have a business card.

- Manage your social presence: Polish your LinkedIn profile. Use a professional headshot. Avoid party pictures with distracting backgrounds. Compose a clear summary of what you do.

- Build a website. In two hours, you can create a simple landing page with Wix or Weebly software.

- Pick a simple name for your company. Make sure it is easy for Americans to remember and pronounce. The shorter, the better. Consider using crowdfunding naming companies to find a good moniker. To avoid a future lawsuit, confirm that the name you choose has not been taken by another enterprise. Have a good story to tell about your company name.

- Apply to be a speaker at meetups, events, and conferences to share your expertise. Have videos and pictures taken of your speaking engagements. Send those to other event organizers for future opportunities.

- Pitch at public events. There are so many in the Bay Area where you can practice.

- Brainstorm business connections you could contact who are already in Silicon Valley.

- Volunteer to organize events and mentor at startups and incubators.

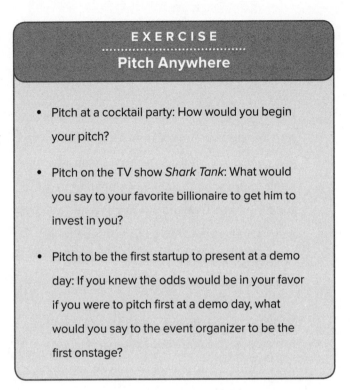

EXERCISE

Pitch Anywhere

- Pitch at a cocktail party: How would you begin your pitch?

- Pitch on the TV show *Shark Tank*: What would you say to your favorite billionaire to get him to invest in you?

- Pitch to be the first startup to present at a demo day: If you knew the odds would be in your favor if you were to pitch first at a demo day, what would you say to the event organizer to be the first onstage?

More Rules for Non-Native English Speakers

- There is an established mode of communication that entrepreneurs use to convey their ideas to investors today. The nonverbal parts include executive summaries, pitch decks (series of slides), and business plans. The verbal can be over the phone, face to face, or during "industry standards" pitch competitions.

- The CEO should pitch. The CEO should speak English. Not perfect English but good enough English to communicate the message and create trust with investors.

Most of the people you will meet at any technology event in San Francisco are non-native English speakers. People with thick foreign accents are the norm. Matt Abrahams, public speaking professor at Stanford, says, "Most audiences are forgiving, particularly of accents."[8]

Marlon Nichols, an Intel Capital investor, offered a similar view: "It doesn't matter where you're from. You have a sound understanding of what it's going to take to drive a successful outcome for the business that you're starting. And I've seen people be very successful at articulating that, that are from other countries. And I've seen people that have done that pretty poorly that are from the U.S."[9]

- Investors expect to read your profile, an executive summary, a one-pager, or a PowerPoint presentation.

- A video demo of your product is a must. It provides an immersive experience to the investor about what you do. It's a great prompt to action.

- Don't address political matters. No matter how much you want to talk about world conflicts, keep it to yourself.

- Be punctual. Arrive at least five minutes early for meetings. Punctuality is a good indicator of how you'll conduct business later on.

The many Japanese, Korean, and Chinese speakers I have worked with come from densely populated countries where it's considered disrespectful to take up too much space, even when speaking. They tend to stay very still when presenting, which is contrary to what you should do here.

Remember to:

- Verbalize explicitly everything you want to say, not just 70 percent of it, hoping that your audience will get the full 100 percent. Don't assume that your audience knows what you are talking about. Explain clearly. There is a Japanese saying, "Hear 1, understand 10," which, as you can imagine, can leave an unprepared audience perplexed or lost. The French, on the contrary, when they want to say 100 things, will verbalize 150.

- In North America, public speaking is an art form. Pauses are good; silences are not. Pausing increases the tension and gets our attention. Too much silence makes us uncomfortable.

- Relax. Don't be so formal. Proper form is quite important in Asian cultures. For instance, there is a correct way to present your business card: with two hands and a bow. But in Silicon Valley, a good pitch is more about a well-prepared conversation than about a monologue. Loosen up.

- Own the room. Address everyone, not just the top people. You are expected to exhibit some degree of extroversion. In North America, it shows leadership.

- Keep it simple. As Zeinab Badawi, the BBC anchor, says, "Speak clearly, get to your point quickly, don't beat about the bush, marshal your thoughts, keep your arguments simple. I am a great believer in complex ideas explained in a simple manner. I would say, think before you speak, think ahead to what you are going to be saying, and try to keep the language as simple as possible."[10]

APPLYING TO AN INCUBATOR OR ACCELERATOR PROGRAM

The 500 Startups program in Mountain View, where I served as a mentor on pitch preparation for two years, receives more than a thousand applications for 30 openings. The three-month program ends with a demo day. Founders pitch in front of a crowd of investors, press, and friends. It's a three-minute pitch.

I see many of the same basic mistakes.

Pitch Me (and Only Me)

Don't send a video to 500 Startups that you have already sent to Techstars or some other incubator program, with the title "Techstars application" or, worse, with the greeting "Hi, Techstars." It looks bad.

Get Onstage (and Get Off)

Say what your company does in one sentence, using two verbs. I have reviewed 20 companies already. I'm tired. Capture my attention right away.

Confess All (I'll Appreciate It)

But don't tell me you have zero customers or users. Numbers and growth are important even if you're still building.

Drop Anchors (Show Me You Didn't Create an Imaginary World)

Tell me about the companies you worked for and the achievements, awards, and patents you may have that will prevent me from hitting the unlike button.

Ask Me to Do Something

What do you want me to do after your pitch ends? Or after I read your application? Don't let me wander off by myself and do nothing about your case.

Video is a very effective means for individuals and companies to engage in a sincere conversation and connect authentically with customers, users, partners, and investors. What is video, really, but a medium for telling stories as a way to convince people of the value of a business?

Videos should be only a couple of minutes long, so you must nail the "get" from the very beginning, not when the credits roll. You have less than 10 seconds to prevent the viewer from closing the window, so the hook has to be very strong.

Get Your Pitch on Video

Pick a quiet location. Avoid recording near a window, with heavy traffic outside.

Choose an area with warm colors or a simple background. Avoid distractions behind you. You may record in front of a plain white wall.

Use natural and bright lighting so that you're clearly visible.

Place the camera between five and eight feet away from you. We want to see you completely within the frame of the shot, close enough to see your facial expressions but not so close as to overpower the frame.

Look at the camera during your presentation.

Make sure the microphone picks up your voice clearly.

Allow the camera to record for five seconds both before you begin your presentation and after you have finished to ensure that it captured your speech in its entirety.

EXERCISE

Make a Good First Impression on Video

Investors accept pitches on video. However, don't send one that is longer than two minutes. Getting it right is critical. What do you have to pay attention to when recording your pitch on video?

- Pick the right thumbnail or preview of your video. That's the first thing people see.

- Look directly at the camera to build a connection with the viewer.

- Insert a caption with your name and the name of your startup on the lower third of the frame.

- Use everyday language.

   Keep in mind that the video is a direct reflection of how you run or will run your business. It needs to have a professional feel.

THE UNSPOKEN RULES: WHAT ARE THE BEST CONDITIONS FOR A PITCH?

Pitch in the Morning, If Possible

Capturing an audience's attention depends on the time of day. A study in Israel of two different parole boards found that distinct breaks in the day made a difference in the number of favorable rulings. Not surprisingly, favorable rulings were greater at the beginning of the day and after a food break.[11]

Like anyone else, investors and businesspeople in Silicon Valley have different attention spans at different times of day. It helps to pitch as early in the day as possible. Investors working on Sand Hill Road get up before 6 a.m. When you enter the popular restaurant Madera at 8 a.m., the strong voices sound like they are starting the second half of their day.

Pitch from Tuesday to Thursday

On Monday, people usually catch up and have meetings. On Friday, they are tired and thinking about the weekend.

Pick a Quiet Spot

Find a corner or location that is less public, with a low potential for distraction, if possible. A crowded room, a train platform, or a busy hallway is not ideal.

Ask If This Is the Right Moment

Investors can be distracted by their own problems. To increase your chances of getting their attention, make sure it's a good time. Follow them on social media. Check the news. Something big may have happened at their firm. If they had a break-in at their house or a family member has died, it's not the right moment to pitch.

Pitch When You Are at Your Best

At what time of day are you most energized? Pitch then.

THE UNSPOKEN RULES: BUILD RAPPORT

Do the necessary research on investors so that you are familiar with their business and can tailor what you are pitching to their needs and interests. Don't ask about what their firm has done but about specific companies related to what they handle. This will show that you've done your homework.

I always encourage clients to find common ground as a way to build rapport. It's about interpersonal chemistry.

"A lot of founders get caught up in trying to follow a perfect template, and drone on and on about their competitors, the market evolution, and so on. They're bored, and it shows," says Sam Altman, president of Y Combinator. "The way to pitch well is to focus on the parts of the business that truly excite you. That will shine through, and it will get the investors excited. Conveying your passion for the business is almost as important as what you say, and it's almost impossible to fake."[12]

So how do you convey enthusiasm?

Be Positive

It's all about the attitude. Smile. Be energetic. Don't say, "I am passionate about what I do." Show me. Emotions are contagious. Others will pick up on your excitement and will become excited themselves.

Show That You Care About Your Product

Share your knowledge about the product. Tell your audience what you like about it. Ask for feedback. Encourage people to share their ideas about your product. Make sure that your pitch reflects your personality and passion, which mostly involves remembering why you started the business in the first place. If you aren't passionate about what you do, no one else will be, either.

Talk About Your Vision

Share what you envision with the audience. Let people see the big picture. But be focused and keep track of the time.

Exhibit Confidence

Don't undermine yourself by saying, "I didn't know what I was doing," or "I had a very bad product at the beginning."

You are expected to show confidence and trust in yourself and your product. Otherwise, how do you expect other people to have confidence and trust in you? Don't be cocky, though. According to Tomas Chamorro-Premuzic, professor of business psychology at University College London and vice president of innovation at Hogan Assessments, "In virtually every culture, and especially the Western world, we tend to equate confidence with competence. So we automatically assume that confident people are also more able-skilled or talented. . . . External humility is not just very important, but very underrated—especially in the U.S. All of the evidence from psychological research suggests that humility makes you more likable, even in the U.S. So that is when people perceive that you are more competent than you think you are, they will like you more. And conversely, when they see that you are less competent than you think you are, they will like you less."[13]

Your message—whether you're looking for funding for a business or pitching a new idea in your existing job—needs to be empathetic. Your audience members want to feel that you have a sense of what it's like to walk in their shoes.

Your message must resonate. A way to do this is by relaying relevant personal experiences. According to Manana Mesropian, manager of the coworking space

Runway, "It provides some trustworthiness and legitimacy to their persona. That already sets the stage for me to pay attention to their product."[14]

You want investors to know that they are placing bets on talented, competent, compelling individuals who will win. That is why crafting an intriguing and confidence-inspiring team story is so important. Don't expect to turn a blind date into a marriage proposal in one go-round. When you pitch, your job is to convince investors to start the process of figuring out who you are and whether you can accomplish what you promise. Don't overwhelm them with PowerPoints. In two or three sentences, state articulately what problem you can solve—not by recounting your entire résumé but by explaining, for example, a relevant experience that led you to start your company.

In the world of high-stakes pitching, it's easy to forget that this is an interaction between human beings. Marlon Nichols of Intel Capital says that he looks for someone he clicks with, as well as competence. "We'd start there and we spend time together, and that's how you build a relationship. Once this happens," he says, he is "incentivized to want to get to know them a little bit more."[15]

Early-stage investing carries great risk, so investors bet mostly on the character of the entrepreneur and whether they can forge a productive relationship with her. "I'm looking to invest in someone for 10 years," says Sean Jacobsohn of Norwest Venture Partners. "Can we work together? In the business meetings, I can see how good she is at working with potential customers or partners. But I need to spend time getting to know her as a person. Can we work together? Do we like each other and like to spend time together?"[16]

Good relationships with investors is key. The path is "know me, like me, trust me." Numbers alone don't make an investment. Funding is a relatively small world, so it's imperative that entrepreneurs be truthful, transparent, and congenial in all their dealings. Burning a bridge with one investor can cut off multiple sources because of their extensive networks.

THE UNSPOKEN RULES: DO YOUR HOMEWORK

I can't emphasize this enough. Not only do you want to practice, practice, practice your pitch, you also want to make sure that you have studied your audience.

"If you don't do your homework ahead of time, you won't understand what areas I'm focused on," says Marlon Nichols of Intel Capital. "I'm a technology investor. If you created a brick-and-mortar company, I'm probably not the right investor. I wouldn't want to waste your time, so don't waste mine."[17]

Adds Jeff Clavier: "We discard random e-mails within probably 10 seconds of receiving and reading the e-mail. A qualified referral comes from the network. If you want to pitch investors in Silicon Valley, because there is so much noise and so many investors, you want to do your homework to understand who are the 10, 20, 50 investors who are a likely target for you, based on what they invest in and what they haven't invested in, because you don't want to pitch an investor who already has a competitive company in his portfolio."[18]

Doing your homework right also means that you need to be prepared to address the question and answer session at the end of the pitch. "If you can go in and know something about what the subject does," says Kerry Dolan, editor at *Forbes*, "so that you can ask intelligent questions, you can get better answers, and you are going to get more respect from the subject."[19]

What could you possibly ask investors? Are there any off-limit questions? Remember, you're interviewing them, too. You want to know what they have to offer. You want to know how they will react when you have a crisis. Will they cut and run? Or will they stand by you and help?

Are You a Good Match?

To build rapport and get a solid sense of who your target audience is—in Silicon Valley, that would be potential investors—gather as much information as you can.

- ❑ Follow the blogs and social and business media where your investor is active.

- ❑ Ask other people about the person you are going to meet.

- ❑ Check whether the person is engaged in social activities or is a board member of certain companies.

- ❑ Study the inventor's past investments or the companies he has been involved with.

- ❑ Read what the press is saying about her.

Learn everything you can. And be confident in knowing that you are prepared. The investor will perceive this as a great show of care, diligence, and true interest and will be more likely to give you informed insights.

What questions could you ask?

- Can you tell me why you invested in Company X and why you hit the wall?

- Based on your expertise, can you illustrate how, as a board member, you helped that company overcome that crisis?

- Could we speak to companies with which the investment didn't work?

- Could we speak with founders fired by the board from your portfolio of companies?

- Which companies did you miss when they pitched to you? Why?

- How much was your last investment? When was that?

- How involved are you with your last three investments?

EXERCISE

Prepare Your Q&A for an Investor's Meeting

Think of other questions you should ask. Write them down.

THE UNSPOKEN RULES: CHANNEL YOUR ATHLETE'S MIND

"The athletic piece—to play any sport at a supercompetitive level, you've got to have a certain amount of drive and self-confidence," says Marlon Nichols, who played on a semiprofessional basketball team in England. "And you can see similar attributes in people, and typically, it's the folks that are going to be successful at anything. They're going to have a strong drive and be determined, resilient. You can just recognize the same qualities in other people, so it helps in terms of evaluating the people side of it."

Training for a marathon, a triathlon, a 5K—the distance isn't the point. The preparation is the key. It's the same with pitching. You want to take into account everything that can go wrong and make sure you are prepared.

"Either you are thwarted by obstacles or you figure out a way around the obstacles," says Keith Teare. "And if you figure out a way around the obstacles, you're doing exactly the same thing as you have to do in a pitch session."[20]

That is, practice, strategize, be imaginative and authentic, and believe that you're the person for the job.

There is fierce competition for investment dollars. Investors want to know that they are funding a winner. Your pitch has to inspire confidence in you.

EXERCISE
Find Your Passion

Take a break. Go for a run. Paint, fish, or garden. Then come back and write down what fascinates you about your product. Consider the following:

1. Why did you start your company? Think about the reasons you opened your business in the first place. Examine what you naturally enjoy or are good at.

2. What gets you excited about your company? Make an inventory of why your business is important to you—and why it is so uniquely exciting.

3. Looking back on your product 30 years from now, what you do want to say you have accomplished?

SUMMARY

Creating a great pitch is not easy. And even if you think you have one that works, it may be in need of fine-tuning. Often, you're too close to the details of your company to remember what will interest others. Or you've described your company so many times before that you start to sound robotic. Successful pitching often comes down to knowing your business and knowing your audience. Deliver your pitch with passion that communicates your excitement.

- Do your homework. Personalize and customize the information for your audience.

- Manage your social presence.

- Find the right time to pitch.

- When pitching over e-mail, establish a personal connection. Mine past introductions.

- For non-native English speakers: your accent or mispronunciations are less important than the substance of your pitch. Focus on what's most crucial to your audience.

- Get to the point quickly. Quantify the information.

- Convey enthusiasm but avoid hyperbole. Keep it simple.

- Establish rapport. Be positive and confident.

PITCH PERFECT: BRINGING IT ALL TOGETHER

ALL THE WORLD'S A STAGE

Your pitch is clear, you know it cold, and you are ready for the toughest crowd. Now comes the fun part: finessing. Practice is fundamental.

Early in my career as a journalist, I quickly learned the importance of preparation—not just of knowing my material cold but of preparing for anything (and everything) that could go wrong. This included scoping out where I might be conducting an interview or covering a news event. You will maximize your chances of connecting with your audience or winning over an investor if you know your surroundings, be it a conference room, a stage, or a restaurant table. You may not always be ready for every curve ball, but you should strive to prepare for as much as you can.

Whenever I do a presentation, I always like to come in at least 40 minutes before the presentation, or even a few days before if it's a large audience. That lets me get a feel for the place and a sense of how far away I will be from my audience. You would be surprised at how many things can go wrong—microphone wires tripping you up, a mic with no sound or bad sound quality, no Wi-Fi connection, no cell phone service or overhead projector—and how easily they can be prevented by some easy advance preparation. Of course you won't always be able to prepare (you see someone you have wanted to pitch in your local fitness club, for instance, and you have to act), but the more you can be ready at any moment, the greater the odds of your success.

When I have an important meeting with someone in a new place, even at a café, I like to check the tables and pick the one where we'll be able to speak most comfortably. I also like the table not to be in a high-traffic area, but rather in a corner, where I'll have a view of the room and the person I'm meeting. Pick the place that has the best conditions to create an atmosphere of trust and intimacy with your subject. Be attuned to the smallest details that will enable you to make a connection.

Learn from the Japanese

The Japanese use spatial techniques that can be applied to public speaking. Japanese courtyards and tea gardens are meant to create the illusion of more space. This technique of arranging the facts in a way that conveys a certain message can be applied to how you tell a story, the narrative frame of your pitch.

The importance of space and organization in martial arts is also a powerful metaphor for delivering a successful pitch. I have been practicing martial arts since high school: karate in Normandy, kendo in Istanbul, kalaripayattu in New Delhi, and kung fu and Krav Maga in the Bay Area. They employ various techniques to attack and to defend yourself, teaching you how to judge and feel the space that separates you from your opponent. Depending on the culture you're raised in, the amount of personal space you find comfortable varies. Looking for the right distance on both sides of the table, for the space between you and your audience, demands some adjustments to create the best conditions for you to deliver your pitch comfortably. This will be different for the entrepreneur from India and the native New Yorker. I often see people doing a number of things that hurt their chances of making these connections and getting their message across before they even start. These seem very obvious but can make an audience feel alienated or uncomfortable. They include hiding behind a desk, chair, or podium; standing too far away from or too close to the audience; and tripping on a microphone cable.

With some preparation, these people could easily have avoided these errors and been a lot more comfortable. This, in turn, leads to establishing a genuine connection with the audience.

Dress the Part

It is also important to dress appropriately rather than being too stiff and formal or too casual. Californians are known to be more relaxed when it comes to fashion, but that doesn't mean that you want to fade into the woodwork. While you probably don't want to wear a fuchsia shirt or bright high-tops, I do recommend choosing colors that will make you stand out, whether it's a bright tie for men or a power color such as red for women. The way you dress should align with the image of your company—and yourself. Gray and drab won't make you stand out.

The Queen of England has been known to say, "To be believed, I need to be seen."

Gather Your Props

Much of the magic of connecting with your audience comes from preparation. If you are about to pitch in front of 500 people, have a pen and paper handy for their questions. Keep in mind that their questions will help you further improve your presentation. If you are presenting in a smaller room and have access to a whiteboard, use a marker pen to note ideas.

For PowerPoint presentations, using a wireless clicker with a timer will help you pace yourself. Always have the screen on your right because our eyes read from left to right. The waistband of your pants or skirt is always the best place to secure the microphone. Have a water bottle nearby in case your mouth gets dry or your voice hoarse.

If you are using a prop, it should add value to your presentation. I once had a client who wore a Fitbit. It was so small that no one could see it from their seats, so we had to show it onscreen to convey its design. Talk to the cameraman (if there is one recording the event) and ask him to zoom in or project the image on a big screen. Just make sure that your audience can see your prop. Otherwise, it will be very frustrating for the people in the back rows.

Don't use too many props. Don't show all the prototypes you have had for your product or its different iterations. We want to see the latest one.

THE POWER OF YOUR VOICE

You may present well and have a winning attitude, but if no one can hear you, then none of it matters. In a video presentation, the image may be blurry and the background may be distracting, but if your voice is strong and clear, your message will come across.

If you are presenting onstage, you have to capture your audience with the power of your voice. One of the most common mistakes I have observed with clients is the pace at which they speak. You want to bring your listeners with you without overwhelming them. How? You have probably noticed that on the radio, when a speaker takes the time to slow down and articulate, you have an easier time processing the information.

It's the same with pitching. When I have executives rehearse their pitches, I give them feedback on the specific places where they should slow down. I also record clients and play their pitches back to them so that they become aware that they are speaking more quickly than they realize, which makes them less effective in getting their message across. I forced one client to slow down by interrupting her until she did. She delivered her message powerfully. Her sentences were shorter and simpler. She punctuated longer sentences and more complex content with pauses. She felt that she was much more convincing. Slowing down is one of the simplest ways to improve a pitch.

We cannot verbalize more than 240 words per minute. The average rate for English speakers in the United States is about 150 words per minute. We tend to speak more rapidly when we are nervous or excited (or from

New York) and more slowly when we are tired or bored. During my workshops in New York City, I advise entrepreneurs to speak more slowly if they are going to pitch in Silicon Valley. If you are speaking on the phone with an investor, write the words "Slow down" on a panel or blackboard in front of you.

Take the time to articulate clearly. Create interest by varying the tone of your voice, whether by raising it, lowering it, or choosing what to emphasize. A monotone will lull your audience and dull its attention. A strong tone is appropriate on stage but may be overpowering in a smaller room. There are cultural differences at play, too. The French tend to lower their tone at the end of each sentence, while Americans are often perceived as loud because their tone tends to rise and travel across a room. They are good projectors. That's a technique that non-native English speakers should use when presenting.

Breathe. When we are under stress, we tend to forget to breathe, and that affects our pace and clarity. At the beginning of each sentence or idea, pause to take a deep breath. Doing so gives your audience time to absorb and process what you are saying.

Embrace the entire room. Make eye contact with audience members in various parts of the room, not just those in the front row.

EXERCISE

Using Video and Audio Equipment

Any digital recording will do, whether it's done on your tablet, phone, or laptop webcam.

Here is a helpful checklist:

- Have a fully charged battery.

- Make sure you have enough storage/memory for a 10-minute video.

- Select continuing recording.

- Test your recording volume. Record yourself for a few seconds and play back the recording to see whether you can hear yourself clearly.

- Use the same parameters for the next recording session.

- Create a folder and date your recordings to monitor your progress.

- If you want to identify your word repetitions, send the audio/video files for transcription. Freelancers can do transcriptions at very affordable prices. Ask for a double-spaced Word document and instruct them to transcribe exactly what you said.

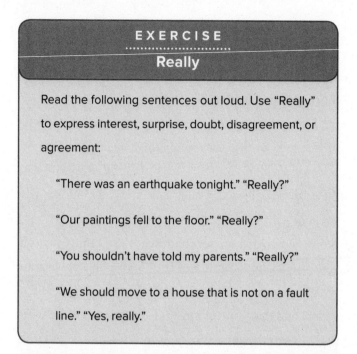

EXERCISE
Really

Read the following sentences out loud. Use "Really" to express interest, surprise, doubt, disagreement, or agreement:

"There was an earthquake tonight." "Really?"

"Our paintings fell to the floor." "Really?"

"You shouldn't have told my parents." "Really?"

"We should move to a house that is not on a fault line." "Yes, really."

EXERCISE
The Nobel Prize Experiment

Print out a Nobel Prize acceptance speech. Read it out loud.

THE BODY DOESN'T LIE

When you attend the Consumer Electronics Show in Las Vegas, you will see speakers who have been trained to look and sound good onstage: a fast-paced entry, warm smile, power posture (open arms), chest out, hands at their sides, and feet hip width apart to anchor the body. Good body language can help a speaker appear more authoritative and likable.

Those who make an impression are likely to appear on camera because they made their message delivery a priority of their communication. In journalism, we call them "good subjects." Using your body to reinforce and support your message is a competitive advantage. "Actions speak much louder than words. So I think that's a very true expression. If you're able to politely, without bragging, communicate to people that you're a person of action, and that your action has led to success in the past, that just sets the context of being able to understand that you are someone who knows how to get things done," says Richard Zolezzi, a mergers and acquisitions lawyer at Nixon Peabody.[1]

How does one achieve that?

- Relax your shoulders, look straight ahead, breathe, and smile.

- Use the space. Take three to five steps laterally, depending on the size of the room. When walking, look at the floor to help you gather your thoughts. Walk confidently.

- When you are sitting in a chair, don't perch on the edge of your seat. Try not to point your knees either at your subject or at the audience. It looks defensive and creates distance.

- When you are sitting on a stool, cross your legs if you are wearing a skirt and put your hands on your knee or your lap.

- When you are sitting on a soft couch, lean on the arm for stability.

- When you are at a lectern, don't grip it or lean on it. Begin there and then move out from behind it and use the rest of the stage. Don't hide behind the lectern.

- If a camera is recording the event, occasionally look directly at the lens, effectively making eye contact with viewers who are not present.

I have seen many distractions on stage that prevented me from focusing on a speaker's message. I have seen speakers hide behind their hair, giving me the impression that they didn't want to be there. I have seen speakers so relaxed that they took off their shoes. And others whose skirts were so short that those in the first row got a show they didn't bargain for. Avoid these extremes so that the audience can focus on your message.

> ### EXERCISE
> ## Learn by Watching
>
> Watch presentations, whether live or on video, and note how the speakers could have improved their body language.

Remedies for Common Mistakes

These are the most common public speaking mistakes that I see, along with little-known remedies to help you give a great performance.

Eyes and Face

MISTAKE: Not making eye contact with your audience. It makes you look untrustworthy, absent, and disinterested.
Remedy: If direct eye contact makes you uncomfortable, look at the spot between their eyes or their eyebrows.

MISTAKE: Blinking constantly.
Remedy: Identify a fixed point in the room and focus on it.

Mistake: Frowning.
Remedy: Smile.

Mistake: Looking up.
Remedy: At the end of each point, look people in the eye.

Mistake: Reading from your notes.
Remedy: Look at your audience.

Hands

Mistake: Crossing your arms. This makes you look defensive and closed off.
Remedy: Put your arms alongside your body. It may feel weird, but this gives you an air of authority.

Mistake: Hiding your hands in your pockets or behind your back. This makes you look untrustworthy.
Remedy: Keep your hands in front of your sternum or navel. It looks commanding.

Mistake: Touching your nose, chin, or arm.
Remedy: Give your hands something to do. Use them to emphasize points.

Mistake: Toying with coins, car keys, or rings
Remedy: Put these in your bag, far away from you.

Mistake: Tapping your fingers. This communicates impatience and nervous energy.

Remedy: Put your palms on a flat surface.

MISTAKE: Adjusting your hair or clothing.
Remedy: Make sure everything is in place before you walk onto the stage. Hold your hands in front of your torso.

MISTAKE: Gesturing wildly.
Remedy: Keep your hands in front of your sternum or navel.

Feet

MISTAKE: Swaying; rocking back and forth; tapping your foot.
Remedy: Plant your feet on the floor hip width apart. Lean forward with one foot slightly ahead of the other.

MISTAKE: Standing in one place.
Remedy: Use the stage. Move toward the audience. Look down to collect your thoughts as you're walking and up again when you've stopped in front of people.

MISTAKE: Turning your back to the audience.
Remedy: If you need to compose yourself, walk laterally.

Verbal mistakes can be corrected because you can hear them, but these mannerisms can't be corrected if you don't see them. You can't eliminate them unless you are aware of them.

Capture yourself on video practicing your presentation or rehearse in front of a group of friends or colleagues and ask for honest feedback.

There are no quick fixes. It takes practice to break bad habits and develop a natural delivery style.

Relax. Take a deep breath. Do large circles with your arms to engage your full body and get your blood pumping. Then count down loudly to clear your voice and your head. Five, four, three, two, one. Begin.

EXERCISE
Work on Your Confidence

Think of your favorite movie character. Memorize one of that character's short speeches. Say it out loud.

Use Your Body to Memorize Your Pitch

While it's important to know the techniques that seasoned speakers use, what works well in delivering effective presentations is committing to memory not only the words but the actions and gestures that you'll be using to tell your story—not only what you're going to say but how you're going to say it.

I once had a client who was very anxious about presenting on stage. I gave him a tip from my martial arts background. When you enter a dojo, you salute the sensei with a bow. It is a signal to your body to be fully present. You forget about the last problem at work, the meeting you need to prepare for, or the deadline you have to meet. Before a pitch or presentation, softly clench your fist as you step forward. This can be your signal to yourself to begin. Or feel free to come up with your own signal. My client's start signal was standing up straight. Another's was opening her arms in a welcoming gesture. Yet another's was putting both of his hands on the table.

Associate parts of your pitch with changes in your vocal tone (to convey excitement), eye contact (when making a point), gestures (to express degree, such as the size of the market), or walking (to show movement or direction). The actions performed by your body as you are saying the words will make the words easier to remember. The physical associations act as a mnemonic device. Muscle memory is extremely powerful. Use your body to help you commit your pitch to memory.

EXERCISE
Memorize Your Pitch

Follow the causal chain from the problem to the market, to the solution, to the team, to the competitors, to the financials, and to the ask. Write the first three words of each sentence on a brightly colored Post-it and stick these Post-its on your fridge or car dashboard. Practice.

Use the Space to Memorize Your Pitch

A 2013 study by neuroscientists at the University of Pennsylvania found that the brain associates places with memories.[2]

Their work shows how spatial information is incorporated into memories and how the brain both tracks location information for spatial memory and records the events that happened in that place.

When pitching, use your brain's geotagging process to help you remember your lines. Associate content from your presentation with what's in the room (the door, the whiteboard, the windows) or a direction (12 o'clock, 3 o'clock, 9 o'clock).

Start with a specific point of focus, such as the red marker on the whiteboard, then walk to the floor lamp when talking about the solution, and look at the subject's watch when discussing the challenges faced by your users.

When giving a presentation, if you suddenly forget what to say because of the stress, simply look around and it will come back to you.

PRACTICE MAKES PERFECT

Practice is one of the most overlooked components of a good pitch. It's what will transform your okay pitch into a stellar one. Incubators emphasize pitch preparation, so startup entrepreneurs dedicate huge swaths of time to rehearse, rehearse, and rehearse until their pitches are perfect. Not all entrepreneurs are part of incubators and therefore don't have sparring partners or professional pitch coaches to guide them or correct their mistakes. But you can practice—and you can do so in front of a select group of team members, colleagues, or friends whom you trust to offer honest feedback.

As you think of how to craft your pitch, remember above all to convey both the what and the why. You are in the business of selling an idea, a product, a business, or yourself. Perhaps you're interviewing for a job or a fellowship. But that doesn't mean the hard sell. It means looking deep inside yourself to capture the essence of what it is you want to convey—and what it is that you can offer that no one else can. What is it that you want to achieve? What scares and thrills you the most—and is propelling you to put yourself out into the world for what you really want? Are you willing to practice, learn, and practice some more to get there?

The Cure for Stage Fright

We all grapple with nerves when we're facing a public speaking situation. Our legs become wobbly, we cannot find our notes, and we forget our talking points. The higher the stakes, the greater the pressure.

A study published by *Cerveau & Psycho*, a French magazine focused on the brain and psychology, suggests that there are effective ways to avoid being paralyzed by stress—and it's all about routine. The more hours you spend performing and repeating a task, the more automatisms you develop that will help you shine on stage and the less danger you feel will threaten its execution. The daily tasks, which are managed by the deeper levels of the brain, are less exposed to stress than others, whereas the new tasks, which are handled by the frontal cortex, are much more vulnerable to stress. "The more you do, the more comfortable you feel," says Bob Donlon, founder of Adobe TV.[3] Preparation is the best medicine. And going on stage as many times as possible is the best way to deal with stage fright.

Practice, practice, practice. You are never prepared enough.

Gemma Craven, former head of social media at Ogilvy New York, describes how much time she dedicates to practicing—a lot. "First, I write a story, the presentation, and then think about how I want to support it," she says. "And then I practice. I read it through three times out loud, making sure that the flow works. And then I will start to memorize sections of it and commit it to memory. I find that going for a run or working out and just playing it back in my head will set it in my mind. And then I'll go back and practice it again." She stresses the importance of being relaxed. "If you're comfortable and relaxed, I think it makes a huge difference. If you're nervous, it's because you're not quite sure of what you're going to say."[4]

Once you have your basic pitch, you need to memorize it so that you can customize it on the fly, depending on whom you're talking to and what the goal of the conversation might be. One of the best ways to practice is to go to a conference and spend the day pitching to 100 people. If your listeners' attention starts to fade, readjust your pitch by taking a different approach, cutting it short, and bringing the focus back to them. You have to convey the same passion, energy, and focus each time you pitch.

Practice Your Questions and Answers

Here's a pitchfest competition drill: two-minute pitch, five-minute Q&A.

As a judge at Silicon Valley competitions, I sat in on both rehearsals and final pitches. If the pitch on stage is a theatrical version of your story, then the Q&A is the live interaction between you and the judges. It's your moment to gauge what interests the investors and what excites most people about your idea.

If a Q&A sounds less scary to you because you can speak without rehearsal, it's important to know that your answers need to be framed as convincing arguments. Here are a few dos and don'ts:

- Don't say, "That's a good question," because everyone says it. Do take a few seconds to think through your answer.

- Don't say, "I don't know." Say, "I will get back to you on that." Take the person's e-mail address and phone number. And do send your answer later.

- Don't be defensive or too argumentative in your response. Remember that investors want to know so that they can share the information with others (their colleagues, partners, or bosses). Don't take it personally. Do accept the criticism and figure out how you can improve.

Now, how do you offer stellar answers to an intense Q&A? Again, preparation is key.

Before the Q&A: Anticipate your listener's expectations and knowledge of the subject. Brainstorm every potential question he may ask. If the subject has participated in public pitch events before, determine his way of thinking and line of questioning. What is he most focused on or interested in? Rehearse, rehearse, rehearse.

During the Q&A: Always cite an example in your answers. Explain why it's important and relevant.

EXERCISE
Rehearse Your Pitch

Print Out Your Pitch in Large, Readable Type, Double-Spaced

Reading from a sheet gives you freedom and space for interpretation, as opposed to reading from the screen of your computer. It allows for more creative handwritten corrections, revisions, annotations, and reflections. I am a strong advocate of getting away from screens. A computer may help you organize your ideas, but a sheet of paper gives you the space to think through those ideas. Seeing something on paper will also give you a better feel for how you sound.

Read It Out Loud

I remember the first time I had to read my news piece out loud to my Radio France Internationale editor. After the second time I read it, he told me that I had done it better the first time around. At that time, I had no clue to what he meant or how to detect what makes for a good news reading. Many years later, I know now that it has to do with confidence, slowing down my pace, fully articulating, and "living" through the piece.

Rehearse each part of the pitch separately so that you don't end up rehearsing the same section more times than the rest and to avoid pitch fatigue. Pause two seconds between related sentences:

(continued)

"Their slide deck was polished. (Pause.) Their story wasn't." By deliberately pausing, you immediately create suspense and captivate your audience.

Record Yourself with Your Tablet or Smartphone

Record yourself practicing. It's a good way to catch and correct your mistakes. First, play the recording on mute to observe your body language. Second, listen to it without watching it so that you focus only on your content. Third, watch it with the sound on to analyze your delivery. Write down what you notice, both negative and positive. When it comes to presentations, there is what you wanted to say, what you actually said, and what you wish you had said. There is no need to beat yourself up. The true difference, once your pitch is crafted, is how animated and passionate you come across. Good posture opens and increases air flow to your lungs, giving your voice more power.

If you want to go even further, have an audience member record your actual pitch. Watch it and make the necessary improvements for the next presentation.

EXERCISE
Pitch Blindfolded

- Do your entire pitch without referring to your notes.

- Do your pitch silently.

Can you get through it without a hitch?

EXERCISE
Watch Yourself

The number one rule of pitching: practice.

1. Practice your pitch on a friend, colleague, or family member. If possible, try to find someone who does not know anything about your idea. Ask that person to summarize for you what she heard. Be attentive to the questions she asks. Write them down.

2. Record your pitch with your tablet or smartphone. Play it back. Answer the following when critiquing yourself:

   - Did I stay within the 60-second time frame?

(continued)

- Was I talking too quickly, slowly, softly, or loudly?

- Was my presentation conversational, or did it sound too rehearsed?

- Did I use filler words ("um," "uh," "like"), a particular phrase, or jargon repeatedly?

- How was my energy level?

- Did I sound confident?

- Did I enjoy myself?

- Was I smiling?

3. If you are presenting at an event, record your presentation or have someone do it for you. Have it transcribed. You will have a better sense of what parts of your presentation need tightening.

SUMMARY

- You are always onstage. Your best opportunity may come when you least expect it—at an airport or in a crowded bar.

- Practice makes perfect. Continue to hone your pitch so that you are always ready, whether you are at a pitch slam, in a formal boardroom, or sharing a cab with a potential investor.

- Use your body to memorize your pitch. Muscle memory is powerful.

- Use the space to commit your pitch to memory. Geotag your lines to remember them better.

- Prepare for a comprehensive Q&A.

- Project confidence through your attire and through your voice. Realize that you'll sometimes need to fake it until you make it. The best pitchers were not born that way. They mastered the skill by being passionate about an idea or project and conveying it with confidence.

CHECKLIST

Mastering your elevator pitch is an art that communicates the essence of who you are and what you have to offer. Here is a checklist of what you need to remember before pitching:

❏ Print out your pitch.

❏ Practice at least 24 hours before.

❏ Visit the venue. Rehearse at the venue if possible.

❏ Make sure all the equipment is working properly.

❏ Dress appropriately.

❏ Practice your pitch again.

❏ Believe in yourself. You have this opportunity.
   Make it matter.

You are ready!

CONCLUSION

....

An executive at a well-known Bay Area semiconductor firm once told me that he and his team had come to expect boring and uninspired presentations from their CEO. As a storytelling expert, I immediately wanted to change that. Nothing is more rewarding than transforming an apathetic presenter into a gifted storyteller: bringing clarity to a message; sharing the passion I sense within an entrepreneur and doing what it takes to enhance it; brainstorming about the value of a product and weaving it into a story no one has ever heard before; and creating stories that travel the world and get to the heart of the matter.

Most of the entrepreneurs I worked with didn't realize that they had something amazing inside them, waiting to get out.

I am very privileged in my work. I get to help a variety of people uncover the elements of their stories. But I am not the owner of their stories. They are.

Storytelling is about people. It's about you. Behind even the most geeky, technical, and jargony of products, there is a person. Behind every product are problems to resolve and struggles to showcase. Our biggest challenge as storytellers is to discover them and shape them to fit today's demanding formats. A good story alone doesn't make the perfect pitch. By simplifying your delivery, practicing, and refining it, you will be able to showcase the biggest selling point of the idea, product, or business—or yourself—and turn the story into a memorable one.

The only rules? Your stories have to be short, true, and personal. A 10-second hook is essential if you are to hold your audience spellbound. What works for an investor from the West Coast does not necessarily work for one from Europe or Asia. Do your research; do your homework. Establish the connection. Stories are not about being perfect. They are about the bumps, pitfalls, roller-coaster moments, and epiphanies in the life of your product. Your struggles and how you overcame them make us root for you because they let us relate to you. Stories connect the listener to your pitch in ways that a PowerPoint presentation or an Excel spreadsheet simply cannot.

What I have shared with you in this book is meant to get you started. Your story needs to be crafted, refined, and practiced. It takes time and effort to think back to your childhood, to the figures who inspired you, and to the breakthrough moments that fueled your drive and shaped your ability to write your own story and chart your unique journey in unimaginable ways. No stories can be improved until they are told in front of many audiences. No stories can live if they are not shared as a means to connect with others. No stories can travel if they are not retold by those they touch.

Practice your raw pitch in a place where you feel comfortable enough to try new things. There are many resources. Attend public speaking meetups. Check with your human resources department for presentation training; join your local university or your business association group. The more you watch other storytellers and hear other stories, the more exposed you will be to elements that you might want to incorporate into your own. Dedicate three sessions of 30 minutes per week to work on your pitch. Look back and measure how your pitch has evolved since you started your venture.

Isolate yourself from the noise. Switch off all your devices. Look inside. It's all there. Begin the process.

NOTES

Chapter 1

1. http://www.pewresearch.org/2007/08/22/two.decades.of
.american.news.preferences.2/.
2. Jeff Clavier, telephone interview with author, April 4, 2014.
3. http://bits.blogs.nytimes.com/2014/08/02/where-tech-is
-taking-us-a-conversation-with-intels-genevieve-bell/.
4. https://medium.com/@munchery/pitch.your.life.2f170
eab933b.
5. http://obamaspeeches.com/.
6. http://greatergood.berkeley.edu/article/item/how_stories
_change_brain.
7. http://www.independent.co.uk/news/science/brain-function
-boosted-for-days-after-reading-a-novel-9028302.html.
8. http://www.newyorker.com/magazine/1975/12/08/the-uses-of
-enchantment.
9. http://significantobjects.com/.
10. http://wornwear.patagonia.com/page/14.
11. http://www.nobelprize.org/nobel_prizes/literature/laureates/.

Chapter 2

1. http://blog.samaltman.com/fundraising-mistakes-founder
-make.
2. Kate Albright-Hanna, interview with author, Deauville, France,
October 15, 2010.

3. https://www.psychologytoday.com/articles/201103/the-inside -story.

4. Nick Kanellis, interview with author, New York, New York, February, 2013.

5. http://thenextweb.com/entrepreneur/2011/10/29/dave -mcclures-10-tips-for-the-perfect-investment-pitch/.

6. https://www.psychologytoday.com/articles/201103/the -inside-story.

7. https://tulane.edu/news/newwave/011110_cooper.cfm.

8. http://www.ted.com/talks/jamie_oliver?language=en.

9. http://www.ted.com/talks/amy_cuddy_your_body_language _shapes_who_you_are/transcript?language=en.

10. http://www.ted.com/talks/jill_bolte_taylor_s_powerful_stroke _of_insight?language=en.

11. http://www.ted.com/talks/ngozi_okonjo_iweala_on_aid _versus_trade?language=en.

12. http://www.ted.com/talks/dan_pallotta_the_way_we_think _about_charity_is_dead_wrong?language=en.

13. http://www.ted.com/talks/lawrence_lessig_we_the_people _and_the_republic_we_must_reclaim.

14. http://www.ted.com/talks/dan_pink_on_motivation? language=en.

15. Richard Zolezzi, telephone interview with author, March 4, 2014

16. George Kellerman, interview with author, Mountain View, California, February 25, 2014.

17. Natacha Ruck, interview with author, Stanford, California, June 11, 2014.

18. https://hbr.org/2013/10/chobanis-founder-on-growing-a-start -up-without-outside-investors.

19. Samantha O'Keefe, telephone interview with author, May 16, 2014.

20. http://thenextweb.com/entrepreneur/2011/10/29/dave -mcclures-10-tips-for-the-perfect-investment-pitch/.

21. http://www.businessinsider.com/shark-tank-best-pitches -strategies-2013-10.

22. https://www.youtube.com/watch?v=AFzPYFmRE-Q.
23. https://hbr.org/2014/07/the-dangers-of-confidence/.

Chapter 3
1. http://www.everycompanyisamediacompany.com/every
   -company-is-a-media-/2010/03/welcome-when-every-company
   -is-a-media-company.html.
2. http://www.paulgraham.com/start.html.

Chapter 4
1. Jeff Clavier, telephone interview with author, April 1, 2014.
2. Sean Jacobsohn, telephone interview with author, April 25, 2014.
3. Jeff Clavier, telephone interview with author, April 1, 2014.
4. Jeff Clavier, telephone interview with author, April 1, 2014.
5. Sean Jacobsohn, telephone interview with author, April 25, 2014.
6. http://techcrunch.com/2014/06/07/the-ascent-of-early-stage
   -venture-capital/.
7. Richard Zolezzi, telephone interview with author, March 4, 2014.
8. Matt Abrahams, telephone interview with author, November 11, 2013.
9. Marlon Nichols, telephone interview with author, April 18, 2014.
10. Zeinab Badawi, interview with author, Deauville, France, October 15, 2010.
11. http://www.pnas.org/content/108/17/6889.full#.
12. http://blog.samaltman.com/fundraising-mistakes-founder-make.
13. https://hbr.org/2014/07/the-dangers-of-confidence/.
14. Manana Mesropian, telephone interview with author, April 22, 2014.
15. Marlon Nichols, telephone interview with author, April 18, 2014.

16. Sean Jacobsohn, telephone interview with author, April 25, 2014.
17. Marlon Nichols, telephone interview with author, April 18, 2014.
18. Jeff Clavier, telephone interview with author, April 1, 2014.
19. Kerry Dolan, interview with author, San Francisco, California, October 28, 2011.
20. Keith Teare, interview with author, San Francisco, California, January 9, 2014.

Chapter 5

1. Richard Zolezzi, telephone interview with author, March 4, 2014.
2. http://www.upenn.edu/pennnews/news/memories-are-geo tagged-spatial-information-penn-researchers-say.
3. Bob Donlon, interview with author, San Francisco, California, Nov 8, 2011.
4. Gemma Craven, telephone interview with author, March 12, 2014.

INDEX

ABOUT THE AUTHOR

 **Marie Perruchet** is the founder of One Perfect Pitch, a consulting firm based in San Francisco. A former journalist and news correspondent for the BBC and other international media outlets, she is a communications and media expert with extensive experience in messaging, storytelling, public speaking, and presenting on stage and in front of the camera.

One Perfect Pitch specializes in helping business executives shape their stories and deliver perfect pitches. As a mentor at 500 Startups, the largest accelerator program in the United States, she helped prepare startup founders and entrepreneurs for demo day, when they pitch venture capital funds and angel investors.

Marie counts among her clients multinationals, tech incubators and accelerators, startup founders and entrepreneurs, and portfolio companies. She also coaches

C-level executives from international institutions. She has been featured in the *Wall Street Journal*, *Marie Claire*, and *Le Monde*.

Born in South Korea, she grew up in France and has lived in numerous countries around the world. She is fluent in French, Spanish, and English and has a working knowledge of Korean, Mandarin, and Turkish. She lives in San Francisco with her husband and daughter. She loves traveling, visiting local bookstores, and all things red.

Follow her on LinkedIn or connect with her on Twitter @MPerruchet #HowToPitch #OnePerfectPitch.

Visit oneperfectpitch.com for more information.